Turning the Hearts of the Leaders Toward the Father

A Journey Through the Book of Malachi

Dr. Lee Ann B. Marino, Ph.D., D.Min., D.D.

Turning the Hearts of the Leaders Toward the Father

A Journey Through the Book of Malachi

Dr. Lee Ann B. Marino, Ph.D., D.Min., D.D.

 Published by:
Righteous Pen Publications
(The righteousness of God shall guide my pen)
www.righteouspenpublications.com

All rights reserved. Except as permitted under the U.S. Copyright Act of 1976, no part of this book may be reproduced, distributed, or transmitted in any form or by any means, electronic or mechanical, or saved in any information storage and retrieval system without written permission from the author.

Unless otherwise noted, Scriptures taken from the Holy Bible, New International Version ®, NIV® (1984),
Copyright © 1973, 1978, 1984, 2011 by Biblica, Inc.™ Used by permission of Zondervan.
All rights reserved worldwide.

Passages marked KJV are from the King James Version of the Holy Bible, Public domain.

Book classification: Books > Religion & Spirituality > Christian Books & Bibles > Bible Study & Reference > Commentaries > Old Testament > Prophets.

Cover and interior photos are in the public domain.

Copyright © 2015, 2025 by Dr. Lee Ann B. Marino.

ISBN: 1940197252
13-Digit: 978-1-940197-25-8

Printed in the United States of America.

Jesus said, "I took My place in the midst of the world,
and I appeared to them in flesh. I found all of them
intoxicated; I found none of them thirsty.
And My soul became afflicted for the sons of men,
because they are blind in their hearts and do not have
sight; for empty they came into the world,
and empty too they seek to leave the world.
But for the moment they are intoxicated.
When they shake off their wine,
then they will repent."
(The Gospel of Thomas, Verse 28)[1]

Table of Contents

	Acknowledgments...	i
	Preface..	1
	Introduction: About the Book of Malachi........................	5
1	The Issue of Blemished Sacrifices and Offerings........	9
2	The Price of Disobeying God and Breaking Faith.....	27
3	Repent From Financial Deception!.................................	57
4	The Coming Day of Judgment and Promise...............	77
	References...	85
	About the Author..	91

Acknowledgements

I want to, first and foremost, commend all the students who are seminary students through Apostolic Covenant Theological Seminary or who have been ordained through SAFE Ministries who were required to labor extensively in the book of Malachi, using the different advances, additions, changes, and editions of this very text. Over the years, I have been blessed to add to my initial study on Malachi, expanding the revelation God has given to me. As one of the most acclaimed texts, I am grateful the revelation contained herein has been such a blessing to all of you.

Secondly, this book would not be complete without thanks to the many apostles I have been blessed to fellowship with over the years. I have learned from many of you; trained many; trained some of those that some of you lead; worshipped with you; preached with you; and I certainly do pray, have blessed you as much as you all have blessed me.

Preface

I never studied the Book of Malachi closely until about six years ago. While I'd read it, highlighted and underlined it in several translations, and passed by passages of it here and there, Malachi was never a book to which I paid much attention. I am not sure for my reason in neglecting Malachi. I believe I overlooked its contents for the simple reason that much of the church also overlooks its contents. Its call to attention, discipline, solid leadership, and divine obedience make Malachi's contents unpopular with many modern churchgoers. In an environment centered around personal self-esteem, getting one's act together is not a popular message in today's church. While I never ascribed to modern concepts that many misguidedly have about the church, I did indeed overlook Malachi because those immersed in some modern ideas never made the book of Malachi a source of inspired teaching.

There is no question in my mind that we, as Christians, have our favorite passages and favorite books. Some passages speak to us more than others. Many find themselves intimidated by long lists of genealogies and historical Old Testament records. Most people like to understand what they read and get confused by various complex passages and translations. We like to be encouraged as we read Scripture. We like to know God is with us, looking out for us, and transforming us to be all we can be. Yet somewhere in there, it's obvious many have made Christianity more about us being who we are or want to be than transforming ourselves and glorifying Who He is. To the world, modern Christianity often looks void of substance, as those who claim its precepts often know nothing more than self-esteem and personal encouragement.

We also cannot deny the mainline Christian community takes their cue from the preachers they embrace. The passages, concepts, and ideas Christians espouse come straight from the mouths, writings, and ideas of their leaders. Many criticize, condemn, even question the state of Christianity today on the level of believers. They try to argue and debate with individuals who only know how to repeat what's been ingrained in their hearts and minds. In the face of debate, everyone arguing about who is right and who is wrong, the result has become total and complete chaos.

Christianity has lost the art of debate and order. Within question of debate, there is also the question of addressing that debate in an ordered fashion. When serious issues arise, who handles them? How are they addressed? What are signs of God addressing errant issues in the church? How does God speak to His people, the church? While we all know God addresses issues in individuals, how does He address matters on a corporate level?

Thus, we enter the book of Malachi. Malachi's approach to his world is far different than the hopelessly optimistic, sometimes vapid perspective which we see today. He is stern, serious, and concerned about the spiritual fall of the nation in which he lives. And in his words, we hear a reprimand, a call to address things we deal with, even now. This short Old Testament book shows how God addresses corporate church disobedience. God squarely places responsibility for church disobedience on disobedient leaders while acknowledging the disobedience of followers, expecting all involved to change. When leaders fail to teach truth, model truth, and live truth, others in the church follow suit. Malachi shows the path of church disorder, starting with poor leadership, and trickling all the way down to every member of the church body. Every leader who is wayward is called back to Him, to follow His ways, that others may follow the ways of God, as well.

Malachi is the uncovering of everything that leaders keep "covered up" in church. While I believe in privacy, leading in error is not something that is to be kept "covered up," because it only continues. The book of Malachi proves disorder comes through leaders who take action against the precepts and people of God. On the surface, such leaders may seem to be doing the work of God, making many strides and advances. In reality, however, they are deceivers, working against God while trying to reap the benefits of appearing to be fully Christian. Such behavior is the secret, clandestine decision to go against God and work for self. In Malachi, we truly do recognize God knows the end from the beginning, the hearts of leaders, and, as a God of justice, will bring truth to light in every dark place.

The church today finds itself in a position not unlike the Israelites in the day of Malachi. With rampant disorder, we need to hear God's call to leaders to stand up as people of God, shape up, and start leading right. God makes known today, much as He did back then, that His standards for leadership have not changed. It is our choice, as His leaders, to stand up and be counted for Him, or to ignore His commands and face destruction.

This study of Malachi, therefore, is a text for Christian leaders. As a Christian leader myself, this lends a unique perspective of God's words through Malachi. Malachi speaks to me on a level of awareness, a constant call to monitor ourselves against the Word's revealed standard for leadership. We need not just see other leaders, but see ourselves; our own areas for improvement, discipline, and greater obedience. We need to see the state of today's church and hear our own call to lead the church more aright in the ways of God.

We must also step back and learn the things of God if we do not know them. Years of disorder mean current leaders may be in error on matters, without even knowing it. We must come in humility to make ourselves teachable, learn what is needed, and review what we already know. We can never think more of ourselves than we ought, and never forget we ascribe to a

Higher Authority on all matters, including that which we teach and how we live.

Many today complain about the state of the church. Many more find themselves unable to agree on how to solve the problems that exist. Let us not be ignorant to hear the Word of God found in Malachi, for in them, we find our answer to begin the healing process for today's church.

Introduction

ABOUT THE BOOK OF MALACHI

Think back for a minute: when was the last time you heard teaching from the book of Malachi? Most likely, it has been a long time since you heard a lesson on Malachi. There are many who have probably never heard a teaching on the book of Malachi. Some probably are unsure of its position in the Bible. Even though Malachi may not be the most popular book for use in Christian teaching, the Book of Malachi is very relevant for our day. For this reason, we must study Malachi to gain an understanding of five key things:

- The state of the church today.

- How God views the state of the church today.

- The connection between leadership and the state of the church today.

- How God addresses the state of the church today through leadership.

- How God calls leaders to respect, revere, and hear Him as Father in their lives, and how that changes the entire dynamic of leadership present in the church

Position in the Bible

The book of Malachi is the last book in a group of 12 prophetic writings classified as the "Minor Prophets." Its classification as does not mean Malachi is in any way of minor consideration or worth, but that the contents of the prophecies are far shorter than those of Isaiah, Jeremiah, and Ezekiel. In most Bibles, the Book of Malachi follows Zechariah and precedes the New Testament Gospel of Matthew. In Bibles which divide the Old Testament sections differently, the book of Malachi follows Zechariah and precedes Psalms.

Length

The book of Malachi is four chapters long in most Bibles. In Bibles with alternate numbering systems, Malachi is three chapters long. The content of Malachi is the same, regardless of the numbering system.

Author

The authorship of Malachi is in debate. Different traditions argue for different authors. Many presume the author to be the Prophet Malachi himself. In Talmudic tradition, the author is identified as Mordecai. The Jewish Targum identifies a third possibility for authorship: Ezra. Some suggest as the name Malachi in Hebrew means "My Messenger" or "Jehovah's Messenger," Malachi is not a proper name, but a reference to an anonymous individual who delivered the message.

About the author

There is nothing known about the life of the first possible author. We know Mordecai from the book of Esther, as Esther's uncle and guardian. We also know Ezra was an Old Testament priest and author of the Old Testament book of Ezra.

No matter who might have authored Malachi, we can see Malachi was a type of a New Testament apostle. As one who spoke for God, Malachi revealed the mysteries of God as He revealed the will of God. He was one sent by God with a specific and direct message. As apostles hold the authority to correct other church leaders, Malachi was sent as a front-liner to correct the leaders of Israel. This reveals to us an important component in the purpose of apostles in these latter-days.

Time written

The exact date when the book of Malachi was written is unknown. Because it mentions the postexilic period (when Israel was under Persian rule), most historians date it somewhere between 568-433 BC.

Who is Malachi for?

Malachi is clearly written to address those in leadership. In the New Covenant, leaders are of the Ephesians 4:11 ministry: apostles, prophets, evangelists, pastors, and teachers. In the time of Malachi, the book specifically addresses the priests who cared for the temple. Today, for those under the New Covenant, we read Malachi to be a word of correction for Christian leaders.

Malachi is not just heralding words to be heard by leaders, however. The words of Malachi are written down for all to read, which means that everyone should take heed from Malachi's guidance. While Malachi addresses those in leadership, Malachi is also of benefit to those who desire to interpret "signs of the times" within a spiritual understanding. While most of the religious world points to outward signs marking the days, the Word of God also depicts effects of the last days on the church. We can't identify the problems present in today's church if we don't know what they are and understand them. For this reason, Malachi stands as a signpost of the origin of error and confusion in the modern church. It also stands as the signpost for its hope, healing, and change. There is no reason to despair when reading Malachi, because it also gives us the ultimate answer and the ultimate promise.

History

The book of Malachi was written after the temple was rebuilt, under the leadership of Zerubbabel, in 515 BC. It seems to be about fifty years after Zechariah and Haggai. Based on Malachi's text, gross abuses were present among Jews in this time. We can see from studying other books appearing to be from a similar time (Zechariah, Haggai, Ezra and Nehemiah) that the Jews of this day returned from exile lazy, slothful, and preoccupied with worldly things. In the midst of this, God sent Malachi as a messenger to call the Israelite leadership unto repentance and back to the proper way of right worship, conduct, and leadership.

Context

Malachi is unique among the Minor Prophets. The book speaks specifically to leadership and exposes a spiritual conspiracy against the things of God. Malachi's call is for errant and misleading leaders to repent of their sins and straighten up, to teach and lead the people of God rightly. Malachi emphasizes the importance of leaders in union with God's precepts for leadership, as leaders influence the people of God in a great way. Leaders can either lead individuals toward righteousness or away from it. For this reason, errant leaders must be addressed. Malachi is as much a call for leaders to repent from wrongdoing just as much today as in Malachi's day. May leaders today hear the word for them present in the book of Malachi.

Chapter 1

The Issue of Blemished Sacrifices and Offerings
(Malachi Chapter 1)

Key verses

- **Verse 2-3:** *"I have loved you," says the LORD. "But you ask, 'How have you loved us?' "Was not Esau Jacob's brother?" the LORD says. "Yet I have loved Jacob, but Esau I have hated, and I have turned his mountains into a wasteland and left his inheritance to the desert jackals."*

- **Verse 6:** *"A son honors his father, and a servant his master. If I am a Father, where is the honor due Me? If I am a master, where is the respect due Me?" says the LORD Almighty. "It is you, O priests, who show contempt for My Name. "But you ask, 'How have we shown contempt for Your Name?'"*

- **Verse 14:** *"Cursed is the cheat who has an acceptable male in his flock and vows to give it, but then sacrifices a blemished animal to the Lord. For I am a great king," says* the LORD Almighty, "and My Name is to be feared among the nations."

Words and phrases to know

- **Oracle**: From the Hebrew word *massa* which means "load, bearing, tribute, burden, lifting; utterance, oracle, burden; a son of Ishmael."[1]

- **Malachi**: From the Hebrew word *Mal'akiy* which means "My messenger."[2]

- **Loved**: From the Hebrew word *ahab* which means "to love; to like."[3]

- **Hated**: From the Hebrew word *sane* which means "to hate, be hateful."[4]

- **Crushed**: From the Hebrew word *rashash* which means "to beat down, shatter."[4]

- **Rebuild**: From the Hebrew word *banah* which means "to build, rebuild, establish, cause to continue."[6]

- **Wicked land**: From two Hebrew words: *gebuwl* which means "border, territory"[7]; and *rish'ah* which means "wickedness, guilt."[7]

- **Build**: From the Hebrew word *banah* which means "to build, rebuild, establish, cause to continue."[8]

- **Demolish**: From the Hebrew word *harac* which means "to tear down, break down, overthrow, beat down, break, break through, destroy, pluck down, pull down, throw down, ruined, destroy utterly."[9]

- **Father**: From the Hebrew word *ab* which means "father of an individual; of God as Father of His people; head or founder of a household, group, family, or clan; ancestor; originator or patron of a class, profession, or art; of producer, generator (figuratively); term of respect and honor; ruler or chief."[10]

- **Honor**: From the Hebrew word *kabowd* which means "glory, honor, glorious, abundance."[11]

- **Master**: From the Hebrew word *'adown* which means "firm, strong, lord, master."[12]

- **Respect**: From the Hebrew word *mowra'* which means "fear, reverence, terror."[13]

- **Priests**: From the Hebrew word *kohen* which means "priest, principal officer or chief ruler."[14]

- **Contempt**: From the Hebrew word *bazah* which means "to despise, hold in contempt, disdain."[15]

- **Defiled food**: From two Hebrew words: *ga'al* which means "to defile, pollute, desecrate[16];" and *lechem* which means "bread, food, grain."[17]

- **Altar**: From the Hebrew word *mizbeach* which means "altar."[18]

- **Blind**: From the Hebrew word *'iwer* which means "blind."[19]

- **Crippled**: From the Hebrew word *picceach* which means "lame."[20]

- **Diseased**: From the Hebrew word *chalah* which means "to be or become weak, be or become sick, be or become diseased, be or become grieved, or be or become sorry."[21]

- **Governor**: From the Hebrew word *pechah* which means "governor."[22]

- **Pleased**: From the Hebrew word *ratsah* which means "to be pleased with, be favorable to, accept favorably."[23]

- **Accept**: From the Hebrew word *nasa'* which means "to lift, bear up, carry, take."[24]

- **Temple doors**: From the Hebrew word *deleth* which means "door, gate."[25]

- **Useless fires**: From two Hebrew words: *owr* which means "to be or become light, shine[26];" and *chinnam* which means "freely, for nothing, without cause."[27]

- **Offering**: From the Hebrew word *minchah* which means "gift, tribute, offering, present, oblation, sacrifice, meat offering."[28]

- **Great**: From the Hebrew word *gadowl*" which means "great."[29]

- **Profane**: From the Hebrew word *chalal* which means "to profane, defile, pollute, desecrate, begin; to wound (fatally), bore through, pierce, bore; (Piel) to play the flute or pipe."[30]

- **Burden**: From the Hebrew word *mattela'ah* which means "what a weariness, toil, hardship, weariness."[31]

- **Cheat**: From the Hebrew word *nakal* which means "to be deceitful, be crafty, be knavish."[32]

- **Feared**: From the Hebrew word *yare* which means "to fear, revere, be afraid; to shoot, pour."[33]

Malachi 1:1

An oracle: The word of the LORD to Israel through Malachi.

The name *Malachi* means, "My Messenger" or "Messenger of Jehovah."[34] As the oracle of God sent with the message for temple leaders, Malachi is God's official representative in the book of Malachi. In this message, Malachi presents an oracle, a direct word from the Lord. Notice the Hebrew word "oracle" has the meaning "burden" within its definition. When the Lord gives a word to a prophet, it is serious, heavy, and a burden of blessing. Prophecy often deals a two-fold blow to the prophet: it is a great honor to be a prophet and deliver a message from the Lord. At the same time, prophets live lives marked by grave seriousness, knowing events before they are to happen. Prophecies are often compared to burdens in the Scriptures as they indicate a released heaviness when one proclaims the message they've received from God.

    Malachi was not just a prophet, but a type of the apostle, long before apostles existed. His work was clearly directed to the leaders; the leaders, or temple priests, were the primary recipients of Malachi's word, with the people of Israel as a secondary thought. In Malachi's apostolic type, we see the serious nature of the apostolic office revealed in his call and task. Bringing forth God's direct revelation, word, and appointment is not easy. Being an apostle should never be taken lightly. We should never confuse apostles with other offices or regard the office as an opportunity to wear a fancy title. Apostles are not called to fit into a conventional spiritual system but challenge the convention of their time and bring forth God's holy call in their wake. One of the greatest tests of a true apostle is how well they handle those leaders serving in ministry under their covering and mentorship. Do those under them reflect God's precepts? Do they adhere to His standards of leadership? Do they lead others well? Do they teach the truth? While I recognize all leaders deal with an occasional stubborn person who insists on going their own way, the fruits of apostolic ministry come forth through how they handle those under their ministry.

Even though many people in church today talk about apostles and being apostles, most people do not understand the major task the apostolic call is on one's life and the way the apostolic ministry looks. If we want to understand the apostolic, the ministry of Malachi gives great insight into the way in which an apostle moves and operates. True apostles will also relate to Malachi's work as the oracle of God. Apostles receive the mysteries of God through His revelation and then reveal those mysteries to the Body of Christ, the church, in preaching, teaching, and ministry work. Beyond order, which everyone speaks of as being a unique duty of the apostolic office (technically all the Ephesians 4:11 ministry offices are called to bring forth order, each in their own way), apostles are called to bring forth structure. In the time of Israel, the leaders were not implementing God's established structure. Apostles, being the first-line defenders in church structure to implement needed structure, discipline, and ministry guidance, will see the parallels between wayward leaders of old, the way Malachi dealt with them, and the way that wayward leaders need be addressed today. Apostles will identify with Malachi's struggle to correct the serious misconceptions present in the church and discipline leaders as needed. Being "sent" means being sent with a message – and, many times, it means that message answers or corrects a problem at hand.

Malachi's oracle provides tremendous insight into abuses and problems existing among the leadership of his day. His work and movements were not haphazard. He didn't just randomly voice every thought he had about things on the internet or blast individuals who weren't doing what he thought they should be doing. We know God delivered a powerful oracle through Malachi, whether he knew the abuses through personal witness or solely through divine revelation. Today God brings forth this same level of revelation through His apostles, sent to correct and reveal to today's church.

TURNING THE HEARTS OF THE LEADERS TOWARD THE FATHER

Malachi 1:2-5

"I have loved you," says the LORD. "But you ask, 'How have You loved us?' "Was not Esau Jacob's brother?" the LORD says. "Yet I have loved Jacob, but Esau I have hated, and I have turned his mountains into a wasteland and left his inheritance to the desert jackals."

Edom may say, "Though we have been crushed, we will rebuild the ruins." But this is what the LORD Almighty says: "They may build, but I will demolish. They will be called the Wicked Land, a people always under the wrath of the LORD. You will see it with your own eyes and say, 'Great is the LORD - even beyond the borders of Israel!'

(Related Bible references: Genesis 25:19-34; Deuteronomy 4:37, 7:7-8; Romans 9:3; Ezekiel 35:9, 15; Jeremiah 49:16-18, Micah 5:4.)

One of the great themes in Malachi is God's consistent love toward us, His people. Malachi reminds us God does not change toward us when we fall away from Him, but it is us who changes toward Him. God gives the example of Esau and Jacob for this very reason: it wasn't God Who changed toward Esau, it was Esau who changed toward God. When Esau sold his birthright to Jacob for nothing more than a bowl of stew, Esau lost far more than just a birthright: he lost a right standing with God because he squandered what had been given to him.

The story of Jacob and Esau has fascinated scholars for thousands of years. Why is it of such intrigue?

This is the account of the family line of Abraham's son Isaac.

Abraham became the father of Isaac, and Isaac was forty years old when he married Rebekah daughter of Bethuel the Aramean from Paddan Aram and sister of Laban the Aramean.

Isaac prayed to the Lord on behalf of his wife, because she was childless. The Lord answered his prayer, and his wife Rebekah became pregnant. The babies jostled each other within her, and she said, "Why is this happening to me?" So she went to inquire of the Lord.

The Lord said to her,

"Two nations are in your womb,
  and two peoples from within you will be separated;
one people will be stronger than the other,
  and the older will serve the younger."

When the time came for her to give birth, there were twin boys in her womb. The first to come out was red, and his whole body was like a hairy garment; so they named him Esau. After this, his brother came out, with his hand grasping Esau's heel; so he was named Jacob. Isaac was sixty years old when Rebekah gave birth to them.

The boys grew up, and Esau became a skillful hunter, a man of the open country, while Jacob was content to stay at home among the tents. Isaac, who had a taste for wild game, loved Esau, but Rebekah loved Jacob.

Once when Jacob was cooking some stew, Esau came in from the open country, famished. He said to Jacob, "Quick, let me have some of that red stew! I'm famished!" (That is why he was also called Edom.)

Jacob replied, "First sell me your birthright."

"Look, I am about to die," Esau said. "What good is the birthright to me?"

But Jacob said, "Swear to me first." So he swore an oath to him, selling his birthright to Jacob.

Then Jacob gave Esau some bread and some lentil stew. He ate and drank, and then got up and left.

TURNING THE HEARTS OF THE LEADERS TOWARD THE FATHER

So Esau despised his birthright. (Genesis 25:19-34)

To some, it appears to be a classic scenario of sibling rivalry, where one son steals something belonging to the other son. While rivalry is an obvious element, it is not a simple case of sibling rivalry at play. We are quick to brand Jacob as deceitful and Esau as stupid. If it was a simple case of Jacob stealing something that wasn't his, God would never have blessed Jacob's life. What we see in Malachi is God's use of sibling rivalry to bring forth what was true all along into reality. Jacob identified the weakness in Esau, recognizing his true concept for the blessing and responsibility of a firstborn's inheritance. He seized his opportunity to have what God established for him. While Jacob's call from God was given unconditionally, it was given to Jacob because God knew Esau would have such great disregard for his inheritance.

In Jacob and Esau, we find ourselves faced with a deep and penetrating question: are we Jacob, or are we Esau? Do we claim what is ours, recognizing how we can obtain it, or do we squander what God gives to us? Too often we disregard the gift of God to us, our primary inheritance, and then wonder where God is and why He is not blessing our lives. When we seek something else and squander the things of God, God cannot bless the result on our lives. It is not that God has disappeared, nor that He no longer loves us; rather, it is that we have changed toward Him.

For Christian leaders, the parallel to Esau would be to despise the new birth, the birthright available in Christ. The new birth is about the obvious with a leader, but it is about more than just eternal life. A leader has the command to take what they have received in the new birth to others. In despising this, a leader despises the essence of what God has called them to do and be through Him. When a leader despises the birthright they have in Christ, it is often complex and manifold. Often underlying every complicated, complex, and involved detail is one main issue: following God is simply not what they thought it would be. Perhaps the reason Esau was so easily persuaded to sell his birthright was more than just physical hunger. Esau had a serious spiritual hunger in his life, a longing for something that was not for him to have. He had an empty void that left him lacking in his life, wanting more all the time, not being easily satisfied, and willing to walk away from things at a moment's notice. We could parallel this kind of longing with modern-day ministers who long for ministry to create something personal for them. Whether they seek fortune, fame, material things, or personal redemption, many modern ministers are simply not satisfied to follow where God leads them in ministry. Simply put, they desire to obtain worldly pursuits. Such leaders distort the Scriptures and misrepresent God to those who follow them. In this, they show no shame, and instead of taking responsibility for such desires, they assign their endless wants to the promises of God.

We also see in Esau the question of how much a calling means or does not mean to a leader. Do ministers despise what God has given them? The priests of Malachi did as Esau did: they spurned what God gave them. Seeking worldly pursuits – and using ministry to do so – is a sign of despise for what God has given to them. If a minister is using their calling for nothing more than gain, he or she does not have the full understanding of what it means to be called of God. In a split-second decision, the choice to embrace or despise sets ministries and lives on an unalterable course.

The story of Esau and Jacob drives home just how difficult ministry can be and that the consequences for our decisions in ministry are often long-lasting and affect more than just ourselves. The choice to do ministry right or wrong is truly ours and our decision to follow God by His grace is ours. When we are in ministry, we have to constantly think of our birthright in all the decisions we make. We must always consider how what we do now is going to affect people and lives later.

The people affected negatively by these decisions show up in the people of Edom. Edom represents the people, permanently affected by the priestly misrepresentations and sinfulness in the ministry. On the current course of events, these people would never be right with God and never inherit His blessings, no matter what they would do. Why would they reap such a punishment? The ways they pursue life, love, and God would be their own. We know from the Scriptures that doing things our way does not work and can never lead to life. The power of negative leadership spans generations as new leaders are trained in wrong ways and continue to pass those errors on to new followers and members.

Here lies the very essence of the book of Malachi. This book is a call for leaders in the house of God to take responsibility for sins and errors. Consequences resulting from actions, or God's required repentance, do not mean God has stopped loving someone. It does mean one needs to love God more and commit more readily to His work, wherever that leads. This proves that believers, especially those called to leadership within the body, play a vital role in their own relationship with God. Leaders still must choose God and His ways, because God does not force Himself on anyone. When a leader's relationship with God is right and one walks as He calls, the fruit of such manifests in the way a leader leads. Leaders will either lead by example or by empty words.

Edom is from a word that means "red," and it is the same basic word as that of Esau. Edom was the nation descended from Esau. It was a tribal group located in the Negev Desert and the Arabah Valley, close to where the Dead Sea is today.[35] The people of Edom experienced great turmoil, wars, and economic destruction over the course of their existence. They could never escape they were founded by one who lived out of God's favor. The same is true for today's leaders. Leaders cannot escape being out of God's favor if they are doing wrong in His sight. Leaders can build works to themselves, but God will eventually tear them down; they can try and pursue work without God, but it will turn to nothing more than waste and rubble. Those who bear God's Name are accountable to Him, especially when they are doing wrong in His Name.

Leaders need healing and deliverance as much as anyone else who has experienced the new birth needs to receive it. Leaders who try to gain for themselves in any form through the ministry will eventually become disobedient. When the disobedient and wicked who claim to be of God are destroyed, it brings awe to all. It stands as a proof-positive testimony that God is real, He is supreme, and He will not tolerate those who bring reproach upon His Name or His people. Whether out of longing, hurt, defiance, or need, God expects His leaders to follow Him, and work out their issues without damaging the reputation of the ministry.

Malachi 1:6-8

A son honors his father, and a servant his master. If I am a Father, where is the honor due Me? If I am a Master, where is the respect due Me?" says the LORD Almighty. "It is you, O priests, who show contempt for My Name. "But you ask, 'How have we shown contempt for Your Name?'
"You place defiled food on My altar.
"But you ask, 'How have we defiled You?' "By saying that the LORD's table is contemptible. When you bring blind animals for sacrifice, is that not wrong? When you sacrifice crippled or diseased animals, is that not wrong? Try offering them to your governor! Would he be pleased with you? Would he accept you?" says the LORD Almighty.

(Related Bible references: Matthew 15:4-8, Ephesians 6:2-3, Isaiah 63:16, 64:8, Jeremiah 31:9, Deuteronomy 15:19-23)

We can see here in the Scriptures that the Lord compared His relationship with the priests to that of a father and a son as well as a servant and master. In ancient times, children were regarded as property, just as slaves were. They were still expected to honor their parents (in this instance, the father) and to obey them. The major difference was that children would grow up to receive an inheritance. This parallels Jacob and Esau well. As bad as Jacob might have been with some of his issues, he knew Who God was in his life. He had many years where God dealt with him and had to handle and soften his heart, bringing him to a place where he was respectable.

It is most fitting for God to ask His servants, "Where is the honor due to Me?" as He transforms leaders from pain to power.

It is even more fitting for Him to ask this question when those who claim to be His servants do not exercise proper worship. As our Creator, our Redeemer, and our Sustainer, those who serve God are to be acutely aware of His presence and influence in their lives. For this reason, leaders must be careful to never show contempt for His Name in any way.

In ancient cultures, one's name represented the fullness of who they were (we would compare it to the concept of "branding" in modern times). It was a representation of their influence, power, reputation, societal status, and morality. Throughout the Scriptures we see reference to the power of God's Name and the command to refrain from using it in vain (Exodus 20:7, Deuteronomy 5:11). To show contempt, profane, or disrespect the Name of God represents doing such to the being of God. Those who show contempt to God's Name are profaning His power, authority, and direct commands to those called as His leaders.

The leaders were also, in a by-proxy way, profaning themselves. Sons carried on the family "name," proving who their father was. If leaders profane the Name of God, they profane their own lives, ministries, operations, and the very work they are called to perform. Recognizing what we say matters (not in the way people often say it does, but in a deeper sense), we eat our own words because they come back to affect us deeply, in multiple ways, in the long run.

But, instead of being honest with God and themselves, the leaders in Malachi question God as to their contempt, instead of accepting responsibility. There are only two possibilities in this situation: either the leaders genuinely did not know God's will, or they knew the will of God and dismissed it in favor of their own. There is a part of me inclined to believe a combination of both was at play here. We have those who truly did not know better as they had been trained by those who dismissed the will of God. If this were the circumstance, why did God still expect everyone to know what to do?

God holds us responsible for what we do, especially what we do in His Name. In the situation of the priests, no matter what their training, they had full opportunity to study the Word of God and learn what God expects. They should not have called themselves "priests" if they did not know or recognize their own calling. The same is true for leaders in this day and age. If today's leaders call themselves something within the house of God, they are responsible to understand that calling. There is no unknowing, only unlearning. In the Lord, none of us can point fingers of blame; we must accept responsibility for where we have ourselves in the Lord. The truth about what someone else does, says, or thinks, is not going to set us free.

God goes on to provide the first example of how the leaders showed their contempt for His Name: they place defiled food on the altar in the form of defiled bread, and they also offered blind, crippled, and diseased animals.

Obviously, those working under the operations of the New Covenant are not confronted with offering animal sacrifices. How do we understand this as a message to modern leaders of our time?

I think we often seek to make symbolism significant beyond what may be obvious. In the case of Malachi, there are many different interpretations of the symbolism present in the book and the meanings contained therein. In the case of the defiled food and blind, crippled, and diseased animals, the relevance is not so much as what was offered, as the condition in which it was offered. As bread (as it reads in many translations) was the main staple and source of food in ancient times, it is most relevant it would be offered to God. Not only did such an offering prove God as the source of all life, it also showed the priority of placing spiritual things above one's very existence. It is no accident that, as Jesus is the Bread of Life (John 6:25-59), such careful requirements were given to pure grain offerings as "types" of this Bread to come (Exodus 29:23-25, Leviticus 7:12-14). If the priests were offering defiled bread, they were using foreign ingredients, incense, fire, or process in the very offering. In the same vein, if the priests were offering blind or crippled animals, they were offering a defiled offering (Leviticus 1:1-17). The animal sacrifices pointed unto the ultimate sacrifice of the Lamb of God on Calvary and therefore could not be blemished (Hebrews 11:9-28). To do such compromised the type of Christ to come. It speaks of offering a distorted version of Christ, whether in teaching, presentation, or doctrine.

Ministers of Christ are all "types" pointing unto the Lord, reminding people of His truth and reality. As living epistles (2 Corinthians 3:3), leaders offer their lives. If leaders are in any way compromising the message, we compromise our ministry type pointing to the reality of Christ present in our lives. Leaders are accountable for the actions they perform in God's Name, as they are here to be the representatives of Christ in this world. There is no excuse for any behavior contrary to a leader's purpose in Christ.

Malachi 1:9-11

"Now implore God to be gracious to us. With such offerings from your hands, will He accept you?"- says the LORD Almighty.

"Oh, that one of you would shut the temple doors, so that you would not light useless fires on my altar! I am not pleased with you," says the LORD Almighty, "and I will accept no offering from your hands. My Name will be great among the nations, from the rising to the setting of the sun. In every place incense and pure offerings will be brought to My Name, because My Name will be great among the nations," says the LORD Almighty.

(Related Bible references: Hosea 13:9, 1 Corinthians 9:13, Isaiah 1:11-15, Isaiah 59:19, Isaiah 60:3,5, 1 Timothy 2:8, Isaiah 66:19)

In verses 8 and 9, God makes a powerful parallel. He parallels bringing a voided offering to a governor with bringing a voided offering to God. Most leaders would never imagine bringing anything to an earthly superior but what they require. It would be unfathomable to bring something considered "void" before an earthly leader. At the same time, many Christian leaders would never think twice about defying God with a displeasing offering. Such defiance shows the true heart of a leader and also reveals a bigger problem. When a leader defies God in such a serious way, they tell the general body of believers they too have the right to defy God. In this way, leaders have the power to encourage defiance as pleasing to God rather than repulsive to Him.

That is why God desires to shut down errant leaders by refusing their offerings. God cannot accept a defiled, polluted, weak, lame, or sick offering. Such a minister must be shut down: their doors locked, and their fire put out so the Name of the Lord may be hallowed, rather than defied, in all nations. God is at work, doing just what He spoke in Malachi, all over the world.

The Bible encourages true ministers to rekindle the gift of God within them, comparing that rekindling to a flame. In the Old Testament, fire represented the presence of God (Exodus 13:21, Exodus 14:24, Exodus 19:18, Exodus 24:17). In the New Testament, Fire is used to represent the Holy Spirit, the passion of God, and the work of God within us through the Holy Spirit (Acts 2:3, Acts 2:19, 1 Corinthians 3:13, 1 Thessalonians 5:19, 2 Thessalonians 1:7, 2 Timothy 1:6, Hebrews 10:27, Hebrews 12:29, Revelation 2:18). Ultimately, fire comes to represent God's presence within us (Acts 2:3, 1 Corinthians 3:13, 2 Timothy 1:6, 1 Thessalonians 5:19). If a minister is not aflame due to God, but aflame due to worldly passions, the flame is useless, only to be put out.

A ministerial offering, given in the Name of God but useless to Him, cannot be accepted by the pure, holy, and spotless God. When we can do better, we need to bring God the best of what we have – not expect Him to handle the leftovers. As a result, God will shut down every false ministry and minister, that the work of God may increase and spread to every nation, and all nations may truly honor God in Spirit and truth, as is His desire (John 4:24).

Malachi 1:12-14

"But you profane it by saying of the Lord's table, 'It is defiled,' and of its food, 'It is contemptible.' And you say, 'What a burden!' and you sniff at it contemptuously," says the LORD Almighty.

When you bring injured, crippled or diseased animals and

offer them as sacrifices, should I accept them from your hands?" says the LORD. "Cursed is the cheat who has an acceptable male in his flock and vows to give it, but then sacrifices a blemished animal to the Lord. For I am a great king," says the LORD Almighty, "and My Name is to be feared among the nations."

(Related Bible references: Isaiah 43:22, Leviticus 22:18-20, Zephaniah 2:11, Psalm 47:2, 1 Timothy 6;15)

God concludes the first chapter of Malachi with further evidence against the leaders who defiled His altar. It is proved here in His Word, once and for all, that the issue of unacceptable sacrifices is not availability. While many would desire to make excuses for such wrongdoing, God makes it clear none exists. Plain and simple, those who have defiled the altar of the Lord did so out of a wrong heart, a wrong spirit, and in pursuit of selfish and lazy desires. They didn't want to deal with the difficulties that often follow those who choose to do God's work. Instead, they wanted an easy way out and sought to use God to achieve their lazy mentality. Even here, God points out such leadership steals and cheats through their false offerings: they steal and cheat as they keep the righteous, or best, offering for themselves. So many today do the same thing in that they keep the best part available for themselves and give whatever is left to God – when they receive all in the Name of God.

Where is our fear of God? Leaders must fear God more than they desire worldly things, more than they want to pursue selfish interests, and more than they want to keep or harbor something that seems desirable. It is not the place of a leader to defile what God has given, or to act against the position God has placed them in.

There is no question we serve a loving, long-suffering, forgiving, and merciful God. There is also no question that we serve a just God. When leaders know better than to do wrong, they must face the justice of God. Here in Malachi we see the call to do just that. Leadership must face up to all the wrong they have done and repent from such wrongdoing. Leaders are to change their wrong ways and do right by God and those they serve. As we continue in Malachi, we shall see more examples of wrongdoing among leadership and ultimately receive God's call for leaders to change their ways and do what is right.

Chapter 2

THE PRICE OF DISOBEYING GOD AND BREAKING FAITH
(MALACHI CHAPTER 2)

Key Verses

- **Verse 3**: *"Because of you I will rebuke your descendants; I will spread on your faces the offal from your festival sacrifices, and you will be carried off with it."*

- **Verses 7-9**: *"For the lips of a priest ought to preserve knowledge, and from his mouth men should seek instruction—because he is the messenger of the LORD Almighty. But you have turned from the way and by your teaching have caused many to stumble; you have violated the covenant with Levi,"* says the LORD Almighty. *"So I have caused you to be despised and humiliated before all the people, because you have not followed My ways but have shown partiality in matters of the law."*

- **Verse 10:** *Have we not all one Father? Did not one God create us? Why do we profane the covenant of our fathers by breaking faith with one another?*

- **Verse 16:** *"I hate divorce," says the LORD God of Israel, "and I hate a man's covering himself with violence as well as with his garment," says the LORD Almighty. So guard yourself in your spirit, and do not break faith.*

Words and phrases to know

- **Admonition:** From the Hebrew word *mitsvah* which means "commandment."[1]

- **Listen:** From the Hebrew word *shama'* which means "to hear, listen to, obey; sound."[2]

- **Set your heart:** From two Hebrew words: *suwm* which means "to put, place, set, appoint, make[3];" and *leb* which means "inner man, mind, will, heart, understanding."[4]

- **Curse:** From the Hebrew word *meerah* which means "a curse."[5]

- **Blessings:** From the Hebrew word *berakah* which means "blessing; source of blessing; blessing, prosperity; blessing, praise of God; a gift, present; a treaty of peace."[6]

- **Rebuke:** From the Hebrew word *ga'ar* which means "to rebuke, reprove, corrupt."[7]

- **Descendants:** From the Hebrew word *zera'* which means "seed, sowing, offspring."[8]

- **Offal:** From the Hebrew word *peresh* which means "fecal matter, dung, offal."[9]

- **Carried off**: From the Hebrew word *nasa'* which means "to lift, bear up, carry, take."[10]

- **Covenant**: From the Hebrew word *beriyth* which means "covenant, alliance, pledge."[11]

- **Life**: From the Hebrew word *chay* which means "living, alive; relatives; life (abstract emphatic); living thing, animal; community."[12]

- **Peace**: From the Hebrew word *shalom* which means "completeness, soundness, welfare, peace."[13]

- **Reverence**: From the Hebrew word *yare'* which means "to fear, revere, be afraid; to shoot, pour."[14]

- **Uprightness**: From the Hebrew word *miyshowr* which means "level place, uprightness."[15]

- **Turned**: From the Hebrew word *shuwb* which means "to return, turn back."[16]

- **Sin**: From the Hebrew word *'avon* which means "perversity, depravity, iniquity, guilt or punishment for iniquity."[17]

- **Lips**: From the Hebrew word *saphah* which means "lip, language, speech, shore, bank, brink, brim, side, edge, border, binding."[18]

- **Preserve**: From the Hebrew word *shamar* which means "to keep, guard, observe, give heed."[19]

- **Knowledge**: From the Hebrew word *da'ath* which means "knowledge."[20]

- **Instruction**: From the Hebrew word *towrah* which means "law, direction, instruction."[21]

- **Messenger**: From the Hebrew word *mal'ak* which means "messenger, representative."[22]

- **Stumble**: From the Hebrew word *kashal* which means "to stumble, stagger, totter."[23]

- **Violated**: From the Hebrew word *shachath* which means "to destroy, corrupt, go to ruin, decay."[24]

- **Despised**: From the Hebrew word *bazah* which means "to despise, hold in contempt, disdain."[25]

- **Humiliated**: From the Hebrew word *shaphal* which means "low, humble."[26]

- **Partiality**: From the Hebrew word *nasa* which means "to to lift, bear up, carry, take."[27]

- **Law**: From the Hebrew word *towrah* which means "law, direction, instruction."[28]

- **Breaking faith**: From the Hebrew word *bagad* which means "to act treacherously, deceitfully, deal treacherously."[29]

- **Desecrated**: From the Hebrew word *chalal* which means "to profane, defile, pollute, desecrate, begin; to wound (fatally), bore through, pierce, bore; (Piel) to play the flute or pipe."[30]

- **Sanctuary**: From the Hebrew word *qodesh* which means "apartness, holiness, sacredness, separateness."[31]

- **Marrying**: From the Hebrew word *ba'al* which means "to marry, rule over, possess, own."[32]

- **Foreign god**: From two Hebrew words: *nekar* which means "foreign, alien, foreignness, that which is foreign[33];" and *el* which means "god, god-like one, mighty one; mighty things in nature; strength, power."[34]

- **Flood**: From the Hebrew word *kacah* which means "to cover, conceal, hide."[35]

- **Tears**: From the Hebrew word *dim'ah* which means "tears."[36]

- **Weep and wail**: From two Hebrew words: *bekiy* which means "a weeping, weeping;"[37] and *'anaqah* which means "crying, groaning, lamentation."[38]

- **Witness**: From the Hebrew word *'uwd* which means "to return, repeat, go about, do again; to bear witness."[39]

- **One**: From the Hebrew word *echad* which means "one (number)."[40]

- **Godly offspring**: From two Hebrew words: *'elohyim* which means "(plural) rulers, judges, divine ones, works or possessions of God"[41]; and *zera'* which means "seed, sowing, offspring."[42]

- **Wife of your youth**: From two Hebrew words: *'ishshah* which means "woman, wife, female;"[43] and *na'uwr* which means "youth, early life."[44]

- **Guard**: From the Hebrew word *shamar* which means "to keep, guard, observe, give heed."[45]

- **Spirit**: From the Hebrew word *ruwach* which means "wind, breath, mind, spirit."[46]

- **Divorce**: From the Hebrew word *shalach* which means "to send, send away, let go, stretch out."[47]

- **Covering**: From the Hebrew word *kacah* which means "to cover, conceal, hide."[48]

- **Violence**: From the Hebrew word *chamac* which means "violence, wrong, cruelty, injustice."[49]

- **Garment**: From the Hebrew word *lebuwsh* which means "clothing, garment, apparel, raiment."[50]

- **Justice**: From the Hebrew word *mishpat* which means "judgment, justice, ordinance."[51]

Malachi 2:1-6

"And now this admonition is for you, O priests. If you do not listen, and if you do not set your heart to honor My Name," says the LORD Almighty, "I will send a curse upon you, and I will curse your blessings. Yes, I have already cursed them, because you have not set your heart to honor Me.

"Because of you I will rebuke your descendants; I will spread on your faces the offal from your festival sacrifices, and you will be carried off with it. And you will know that I have sent you this admonition so that My covenant with Levi may continue," says the LORD Almighty. "My covenant was with him, a covenant of life and peace, and I gave them to him; this called for reverence and he revered Me and stood in awe of My Name. True instruction was in his mouth and nothing false was found on his lips. He walked with Me in peace and uprightness, and turned many from sin.

(Related Bible references: Deuteronomy 28:3-15, Exodus 29:14, 1 Kings 14:10, Numbers 25:10-13, Ezekiel 34:25, Deuteronomy 33:8-10)

The second chapter of Malachi opens with a clear command for the leaders, as well as a stern warning about what will come to those who do not change their ways. Through Malachi, God reveals the plan to send a curse upon those who insist on abusing God's ministry in their selfish pursuits. God specifically makes mention of the leader's blessings: the blessings of the unrepentant priests will also be cursed.

Many ministers today challenge the notion that God is in the business of correction. They theorize, often without any theological defense at all, that God is simply doing a positive, rather than what they deem as a negative, thing in the church today. They teach that if God is unhappy with someone, He will somehow let them know directly and won't involve anyone else in the process. Whether or not someone hears the message, however, becomes a matter of great debate. According to such individuals, the discernment of God's judgment is only about results. By these assessments, people only discern God's judgment upon a minister if their ministry fails to grow, fails to gain many converts, or fails to produce what a specific individual deems as worthy "fruit."

Then there are leaders who believe God is all about correction, right until the correction comes their way. When faced with correction, they grow indignant and refuse to accept what God is saying to them through their leader. Suddenly all the things they see in other leaders, they fail to see in themselves.

The "fruit" standards of such judgments are worldly ones. They defend a minister who may be theologically inaccurate, unprepared, or untrained (even if it is they themselves) because they are popular with many people or seem likeable. Ministries with little substance, worldly visions, improper concepts of Jesus, and misleading teachings are given more credibility over smaller ministries that may labor to present truth and the ultimate balance between discipline and encouragement. This favoritism of false ministries is given simply because such ministries are bigger, flashier, and seem to offer more of what someone wants to hear.

The leaders of Malachi's day were clearly popular with the people. The priests had people who regularly came to the temple with their offerings and provided tithes so the leaders could live. They had power and influence to control how an entire generation approached God. Their popularity was not a reflection that they taught truth, because they clearly did not teach God's truth! Such is true today. There may be power in numbers, but truth does not always lie there. Just because a leader can command an audience does not make that leader truthful or in step with God's Kingdom.

I am sure Malachi's message to the leaders of his day was an unwelcome one. It wasn't uplifting, it wasn't positive, and it didn't "feel good" to those who had to hear it and then repent. Even though Malachi's message may not have been fun, that doesn't change the fact it was needed. Through Malachi, God brought the priests face-to-face with a reality they could not run or hide from. God knew their actions. God knew what they were doing, thoroughly disapproved of their actions, and it was He Who was putting an end to their ministries.

We must grow beyond the concept that blessing is always in a sense of material gain. Proverbs 10:22 reminds us:

The blessing of the LORD brings wealth, and He adds no trouble to it. (KJV)

When the Lord provides for us, it brings no sorrow. IRS investigations, loss of funds, tainted or dirty money, and questionable financial ties are signs of trouble, not of God's blessing. The world is full of people who obtained money through dishonest and underhanded means. Their gain is not from God and comes with a heavy and high sorrowful price. Even leaders in the church ascribe every gain they receive as being from God, failing to realize the origin of wealth is as relevant as the need it provides.

In the blind ambition of this world, it is not uncommon for a minister to ascribe every misgiving, loss, or negative circumstance to the devil's influence. There is no question the devil does indeed work against believers, and can work to cause specific snare, destruction, or despair to those who work in the harvest. This having been said, believers – both leaders and non-leaders – must begin to recognize God's role in loss as well as in gain. In the modern church, many ascribe loss to Satan and gain to God, no matter what the purpose of said loss or gain may be. As believers, we must move beyond this mentality and recognize more is not always what we need to get where God would have us go.

Loss teaches us things about ourselves and reveals where we are lacking in our lives. Loss reveals weaknesses, personal idolatries, issues of necessary correction, and areas in need of improvement. While excessive gain can bury us and our issues, loss can reveal to us deeper spiritual matters pertaining to our relationship with God, self, and others. When major loss comes to our lives, especially as pertain to spiritual matters, we should never assume satanic attack. What we should do is step back and hear God's voice about the situation. While we may not hear what we might desire, we will hear a guiding revelation to the place God desires us to be.

Our current era of leadership merits the correction of God for its gross abuses. All modern leadership abuses can be paralleled to those voiced in the book of Malachi. God is still correcting individuals through those He sends to carry the message of correction in this day and age. We must always remember God's correction brings us life, not destruction. God does not correct leaders to destroy their lives but corrects us so we may live fully edified in Him. When leaders are edified in Him, they can then lead others to Him and edify those in Him. Correction is as much a part of edification as giving words of encouragement.

So why would the blessings of leaders be specifically mentioned as something to be cursed in the book of Malachi? Why wouldn't God simply put a curse on their ministries, but let them keep whatever blessings they had? The Scriptures teach us blessings are things that come upon our life specifically from God's divine intervention. It is important that ministers understand this precept. Everything genuinely good (not things that just seem good but really are not) we have in this life comes from God, Who sees to it that our needs are met. Blessings are always part of the unmerited favor of God, as God does not have to bestow anyone with anything in this life. Believers can, however, do things to cooperate with the grace of God, and bring it to our lives in an abundant way. We can also do things to frustrate His grace and, therefore, drive the blessings of God away (Proverbs 10:6, John 1;16). For this reason, blessings are a part of the inheritance of the righteous. They are a part of seeing God at work in our lives, and they bear a powerful testimony that God is with us, working for us. For the unrepentant priests to reap and keep blessings in their lives would confuse the congregation. If this had happened, the congregation would have thought the priests were receiving good and were therefore doing what was pleasing to God. As we can see from later verses in chapter 2, it is obvious the blessing of the priests caused others to engage in disobedience, in the pursuit of the blessings the priests had received.

We can see in the Bible how the blessings of God fell upon future generations because of the great example an individual might set (Genesis 12:3, Genesis 49:25, Psalm 3:8). We also see God's faithfulness to multiple generations because someone saw fit to sow the seeds of righteousness. At the same time, we also see that to whom much is given, much is required (Luke 12:48, 1 Corinthians 4:2). If God gives us much, He expects to receive much from us through praise, worship and obedience. More than anything, through their praise, worship, and obedience, God expects leaders who receive much to be an example.

Just as we see individuals who were the root of many generations of blessing, we also see individuals who were the root of many generations of cursing (Joshua 9:23, Proverbs 3:33, Isaiah 24:6). It is for this reason we see examples of individuals in the Bible who were killed by an entire assembly for wrongdoing. In this single act, the entire generation took a stand against specific evil so they could continue to reap blessings rather than incur a curse through sinful influence (Leviticus 24:15-16). Cursing is the removal of blessing. In cursing, God removes His hand of protection and well-doing to stand aside and allow the consequences of personal sinfulness. Here in Malachi, we see God's presentation of just that. If the errant priests refused to repent and change their ways, they would reap the harvest of their sinfulness in its full consequence down through multiple generations.

The covenant of Levi is mentioned here because the

priesthood of the Old Covenant was carried through the tribe of Levi (individuals known as the Levites). In studying more deeply from the Scriptures and historical information about the Levitical covenant, we learn the following:

- The Levites were the only Israelite tribe who did not receive a land inheritance. The reason for this, according to the Scriptures, is because:

    ...The Lord God of Israel Himself is their possession (Joshua 13:33).[52]

- The tribes with a land inheritance were expected to pay tithes to God, given through the Levites. This tithe covered the care and living of the Levites.[53] As a side note to this fact, the Levites also tithed, with their tithes going to the High Priest.

- The job of the Levites was to serve in the temple. The Levitical Aaronite priesthood served as priests in the wilderness tabernacle and later in the Jerusalem temple. The other Levites (which were also known as the Gershonites, Kohathites, and Merarites) performed other duties in the temple. The principle duties of the Levites included offering sacrifices on behalf of the people, singing Psalms during temple services, construction and maintenance work on the temple, serving as guards, teaching, and serving as judges to maintain the cities of refuge.[54]

- The Levites earned their great status by standing up in battle for the Lord. They killed three thousand of the unrighteous who were involved in the worship of the golden calf while Moses was on Mount Sinai. Their stand was to prevent other nations from disrespecting the Name of God, as the Israelites created a mockery of God by worshipping a false god. The Levites were a stellar example of the choices we sometimes have to make between obeying God or enjoying status among families, friends, and neighbors (Exodus 32:27-29).

It is obvious from this examination that the Levites were blessed because of their honor and obedience to God, which was put to the test in the wilderness. They proved righteous and received the blessings of God for their obedience many times over. With God as their inheritance, the Levites had the great honor of eternal rewards reaped from temple service, priestly intercession, and God's provision for their continual care. Such care was not extended to the other tribes in the special way it was to the Levites. We can parallel the same type of blessing for those who work in God's service today, living with God as their inheritance and possession:

- God will provide for the needs of leaders. While they may not see the same type of inheritance those in the world receive, the inheritance God's leaders receive from the Lord will be eternal. These needs will be met as the system of tithes and offerings is upheld in God's Kingdom.

- Christian leaders have the duty to serve in God's ministry as good stewards of the New Covenant. It is the job of leaders to lead in right worship pleasing to God, sing Psalms of praise to God, teach and preach, provide refuge to those in need, perform necessary construction and maintenance on the church through right teaching and correction, and serve as guards against all that is founded upon Christ, the chief Cornerstone of our faith (Ephesians 2:20).

- The covenant of Levi, as we can see in Malachi, was one of life and peace. Leaders are too called to preach life and peace as perfected through the Gospel of Jesus Christ. We could classify this as a covenant God makes with all leadership who work in His Name.

- This covenant calls for reverence among all who walk within it, for those who walk in it must herald the same reverence and respect for God's Name and seeing it honored that the Levites first established.

- Leaders must proclaim what is true, and nothing false can come from their mouths, as we know from the Scriptures that blessing and cursing cannot come forth from the same mouth (James 3:10-11). Leaders must live in the truth, walking in peace and righteousness, and through a life witness and ministry, turn many from sin.

Herein is the precise reason cursing was to come upon the priests and their descendants: rather than uphold the Levitical covenant, they led people into disorder. Such conduct cannot reap blessing.

Malachi 2:7-9

"For the lips of a priest ought to preserve knowledge, and from his mouth men should seek instruction—because he is the messenger of the LORD Almighty. But you have turned from the way and by your teaching have caused many to stumble; you have violated the covenant with Levi," says the LORD Almighty. "So I have caused you to be despised and humiliated before all the people, because you have not followed My ways but have shown partiality in matters of the law."

(Related Bible references: Numbers 27:21, Deuteronomy 17:8-11, Galatians 4:14, Jeremiah 18:15, Deuteronomy 1:17, Nehemiah 13:29, 1 Samuel 2:30, 1 Timothy 5;21, James 3:1-12)

In keeping up with the Levitical covenant, leaders have the job to preserve the knowledge of God in their teachings. This means God's leaders have the responsibility to acquire that knowledge for themselves personally. This is so it may become a literal part of who they are and an integral part of their ministerial speech. We learn in the Scriptures that God's people die due to lack of knowledge (Hosea 4:6). This death results because an individual does not come to have the saving knowledge of God and His life in Christ. This demands leaders educate themselves in the things of God, that they may proclaim the life-saving Gospel of God with power and truth (Romans 10:14-15). We are to use our tongues and our mouths wisely, carefully choosing our words, echoing the principles of teachers in James 3:1-12.

God makes it clear the leaders of Malachi's day were not proclaiming the covenant of life and peace but were causing individuals to stumble by their teachings. The root of this problem is found in leaders who turn away from God's ways of leadership and turn instead to other things. Instead of applying the fullness of the law to all involved, including themselves, they created a concept of partiality, observing what would benefit them and discarding the rest.

Once again, we find this to be a common issue among leaders today. To misrepresent the Gospel and cause others to stumble from a false representation breaks the Levitical covenant. If leadership breaks the covenant, the people under those leaders are no longer separated for God and the leaders are no longer founded upon the precepts of the original Levites. God is, therefore, no longer obliged to care for, protect, or guard such leaders as His own because they have broken the covenant they were anointed to uphold. The leaders then find themselves humiliated and despised, left with no blessing, no ministry, and nothing they have sought to gain through ministry, before the entire church.

While people can scoff at ministerial scandals and write them off as Satanic attacks, the reality is that such humiliation, brought about in front of all nations, congregations, and people, is God's uncovering of the sinful, counter-covenant ways of errant leadership. Satan does not expose sin; it is his way to conceal it, letting it grow and destroy the church. It is God Who exposes sin, that all may be aware of what goes on, and make their own choices accordingly to either follow God's ways to life or those of men, which lead to death and destruction.

One of the biggest ways leaders teach against God's precepts is to teach a false gospel of partiality. Teaching a belief about partiality indicates one applies only certain precepts of the Scriptures to certain believers, while failing to uphold the entire Word of God for everyone. While this false teaching manifests in many ways, we see it manifests in some of the ways listed below quite regularly:

- Teaching financial wealth is a measure of one's faith. While there is no question that God prospers believers, the manifestation of God's prosperity may not always come in material ways.

- Teaching poverty is a curse from God and, therefore, the poor and needy don't have enough faith to be pleasing to God (i.e., if they were in God's will, they would be wealthy).

- Teaching God favors political nations one over another and guides nations into wars with other nations. This also manifests in believing God "punishes" poorer nations through famine, hardship, toil, destruction, or natural disasters.

- Teaching famous leaders are of note because they are teaching the truth, and smaller ministries who cannot afford showy ministries are not teaching as much truth; if they were teaching more truth, they would be on television or have more followers.

- Teaching men are superior to women due to Eve's deception in the garden. While many different philosophies abound about the inequalities of the sexes, many in the church apply one set of rules for believing males and another set of rules for believing females, which almost always treat the women as if they are responsible for all sin, still living in sin, or unable to do anything to overcome sin. Men are not given enough responsibility for their personal conduct, while women are given responsibility for the personal conduct of the whole world.

- Teaching any group is superior to another group because of one's race.

Showing partiality toward certain people is strictly forbidden in both the Old and New Covenants. God is no respecter of persons (Acts 10:34)! The same saving power of life and peace is available to all who will come to God in humility and repentance. If leaders are to teach the true knowledge of God, they are to teach all who come as they realize the Gospel is for everyone who shall come and call upon the Name of the Lord to be saved (Joel 2:32).

Malachi 2:10-16

Have we not all one Father? Did not one God create us? Why do we profane the covenant of our fathers by breaking faith with one another?

Judah has broken faith. A detestable thing has been committed in Israel and in Jerusalem: Judah has desecrated the sanctuary the LORD loves, by marrying the daughter of a foreign god. As for the man who does this, whoever he may be, may the LORD cut him off from the tents of Jacob —even though he brings offerings to the LORD Almighty.

Another thing you do: You flood the LORD's altar with tears. You weep and wail because He no longer pays attention to your offerings or accepts them with pleasure from your hands. You ask, "Why?" It is because the LORD is acting as the witness between you and the wife of your youth, because you have broken faith with her, though she is your partner, the wife of your marriage covenant.

Has not the LORD made them one? In flesh and spirit they are His. And why one? Because He was seeking godly offspring. So guard yourself in your spirit, and do not break faith with the wife of your youth.

TURNING THE HEARTS OF THE LEADERS TOWARD THE FATHER

"I hate divorce," says the LORD God of Israel, "and I hate a man's covering himself with violence as well as with his garment," says the LORD Almighty.
So guard yourself in your spirit, and do not break faith.

(Related Bible references: 1 Corinthians 8:6, Job 31:15, Jeremiah 9:4-5, Ezra 9:1-2, Nehemiah 13:29, Proverbs 5:18, Proverbs 2:17, Matthew 19:4, Genesis 2:24, Ezra 9:2, 1 Corinthians 7:14, Deuteronomy 24:1, Matthew 5:32, Genesis 1:1, Matthew 19:6-8)

Malachi 2:10 reaffirms God's message is open to all. Because we have only one Father, Who is God, it is not the place of Christ's Body to be divided by its leadership. We don't serve many gods, we serve only one. It is the same God working through those with gifts different from ours. For this reason, God calls for unity among those who claim to be His own.

The question, "What is unity?" has plagued Christians for centuries. Often, we consider unity a matter of total and complete agreement on all things of life. Others consider unity to be a matter of having a singular leader on earth, and mirroring the same content and ritual, down to every little detail, in every single church. Many believe the question of unity is answered by a sense of denominationalism, where an earthly leader or group of leaders sits down and sets forth what they think their individual group should believe. Still others believe unity is achieved in accepting anyone, regardless of belief, without any standard for truth.

Today's church reflects this full variance of beliefs about unity. While many fall into extreme categories, most are somewhere in between, very confused about what they themselves believe while trying to figure out just what it means to be unified. It does not help that modern leaders are as confused and dis-unified as the congregations they oversee. Failing to recognize unity comes through Christ – and manifests through a spirit of decency and order within the church (1 Corinthians 14:40) – people are greatly lacking unity. Instead of walking in unity, they walk in selfish idolatry.

As much as we may talk about unity today, unity is not a

central core of most theological or Bible training programs. Unity is seldom discussed between covering ministers and those they cover. It is spoken only hypothetically, as an idea rather than a reality. What we fail to realize is the opposite of unity is idolatry. When the church is walking in disunity, the church itself is putting its own wants, feelings, opinions, thoughts, and beliefs above those of Christ. The foundation of such rests in leaders who seek to accomplish for themselves rather than for Jesus Christ.

The influence of worldly desires, cares, and interests is perhaps the greatest threat to Christian unity. These worldly pursuits always lead away from unity, and into idolatry. When the church walks in the flesh, we walk in an automatic spirit of division. If one studies the history of denominations, every single fraction in history has come about because someone is walking in the flesh. Whether it is the originating denomination or those forging ahead to establish their own, someone's walk in the flesh caused an entire following of people to break faith with God. The history of Christian divisions proves the powerful role leaders play in the lives of Christian congregation members. If the leaders stand united, and fail to break faith, congregation members likewise will respond by standing united on the essential matters of faith.

I certainly do not seek to imply Christians should remain under abusive or errant leadership. It is not disunity to leave a controlling or abusive leader, as we will see later in Malachi 2. It is also a false sense of unity to remain under such a leader, thinking one is staying for the sake of unity. In order to understand the focus behind unity and how we are united in Christ, we must understand the essentials of faith.

Embracing those who are in the essentials of faith – and, in the process, refusing to break faith – means we must understand the essentials of faith which are the foundation and determination of such unity. The essentials of faith which determine Christian unity are found in Ephesians 4:1-32:

- Live a life worthy of the calling we have received in Christ. (Ephesians 4:1)

TURNING THE HEARTS OF THE LEADERS TOWARD THE FATHER

- Remain humble and gentle. (Ephesians 4:2)

- Be patient with one another, bearing with one another in love. (Ephesians 4:2)

- Keep the unity of the Spirit through the bond of peace. (Ephesians 4:3)
- Belief in one Body. (Ephesians 4:4)

- Belief in one Spirit, the Holy Spirit of God. (Ephesians 4:4)

- Emphasize the calling to one hope. (Ephesians 4:4)

- Belief in one Lord, Jesus Christ. (Ephesians 4:5)

- Belief in one faith, rather than many faiths. (Ephesians 4:5)

- Belief in one baptism, symbolic of dying to self and rising to new life in the new birth. (Ephesians 4:5)

- Belief in one God and Father of all, Who is over all and through all and in all. (Ephesians 4:6)

- Belief in the grace of God, given to each one as Christ has given it. (Ephesians 4:7)

- Belief in the spiritual gifts of God, given to edify the church of God. (Ephesians 4:7)

- Belief in the resurrection of Jesus Christ. (Ephesians 4:7-10)

- Belief in the five-fold ministry as God's given appointment for leadership within the church, serving the purpose of preparation for works of service, church edification, bring about unity in the faith, knowledge of the Son of God, and the maturity of the Body of Christ until the time when Jesus Christ returns. (Ephesians 4:11-16)

- Belief in the need for maturity in the Body of Christ. (Ephesians 4:13-16)

- Understand the importance of the new birth, having come out of a former life of sin (darkness) and now living in the life of Christ (light). (Ephesians 4:17-24)

- Come to an understanding of God's righteousness and holiness, and the importance of living in both as believers. (Ephesians 4:20-24)

- Conduct one's self in truth and honesty, having changed one's mind to the conformity of Christ, controlling emotions and impulses for the glory of God, and living socialized with all human beings. (Ephesians 4:17-27)

- Be productive in one's life, not forgetting to do good to others. (Ephesians 4:28)

- Speak wholesome and edifying words, seeking to build others up rather than tear others down. (Ephesians 4:29)

- Do not grieve the Holy Spirit of God, understanding the Holy Spirit to be God's seal, marking His people, and establishing us as the Lord's for the day of redemption. (Ephesians 4:30)

- Live without bitterness, raging anger, brawling, and other unseemly emotional conduct, and live instead in compassion and forgiveness, recognizing the forgiveness we have received through Jesus Christ. (Ephesians 4:31-32)

These essentials of faith help us to determine true Christians from counterfeits and to encourage, edify, and build one another up in all the matters that uphold us as believers. The essentials of faith remind us of all we know to be true. They stand as a great sign of all we place our faith in and let us know we will reap the full promises of God which we hope in as we proclaim His message (Ephesians 4:1-32). They also give us a clear statement of who we are to unite with, and in what.

False ministers walk in the dramatic. Too many ministers regard ministry as a big show, believing if they cry enough, flail their arms enough, throw themselves on the altar enough, scream enough, and fall down on the floor enough, people will believe they are sincere. They love to come to church and stir emotions, putting on a big display for everyone to see. Behind this there is no more than a dramatic act, designed to play with people's minds and produce blind followers. Displaying a false sense of sorrow and humility over the matters which grieve God may fool human beings but will never fool God. Many in the church today display grand gestures that seem to display sorrow over disunity, matters of covenantal break, and relationship issues. If we truly look at the state of the church today, how many people are genuine in their displays of sorrow? It is one thing to come to church, act dramatically, and put on a great show before the Lord, but it is another thing entirely to genuinely institute change in one's life. Too often we make covenant about a dramatic show, and not nearly enough about relationship with God. How, in recognizing our faith as covenant, do we break faith?

As we continue in Malachi, we learn the way people break this essential faith: by marrying the daughter of a foreign god. What does this mean to us, and how do we understand this? Naturally not many Christian leaders pursue relationships with spouses of religions other than those appearing Christian, at least on the surface. This means we must pursue this passage further to understand its full meaning.

The Scriptures sometimes compare the relationship between God and His people to be one of marriage (Isaiah 54:5, Jeremiah 3:14-20, Hosea 2:1-16). The Church itself is pictured as a marital relationship, with Christ as the husband of the church (Ephesians 5:25-32, Revelation 19:7). This is because God and

His people exist in relationship together by covenant. A covenant, according to the *American Heritage Dictionary*, is:

1. A binding agreement; a compact.
2. Law; a. A formal sealed agreement or contract. b. A suit to recover damages for violation of such a contract.
3. In the Bible, God's promise to the human race. [55]

While this is a comprehensive definition, if we study the etymology of the word provided in the dictionary, we learn that the word "covenant" originally comes from an Old French form of the present participle verb *convenir*. This word means "to agree."[56]

We find, through the definition above, a covenant is an agreement between two parties. In the case of the Scriptures and of faith, a covenant is an agreement made between God and humanity, or specifically, the humanity that chooses to follow God. In Christianity, we accept God's salvation and, in living in His freedom, we accept His spiritual power and saving grace to lead holy, sanctified lives. We work with God, not for our salvation as that was won on the cross by Christ, but as partners in the covenant we've made with Him. We can cooperate with all He has given us as a part of the covenant promise, or we can reject the promise in full or in part.

Marriage is also used as an image of covenant because of the great intimacy, both physical and spiritual, purposed to exist between spouses. Spouses agree to live with one another and to share oneness that does not present in other earthly relationships in the same way (Genesis 2:24, Ephesians 5:31). The marital relationship, as we see in the garden, was one destined to bear fruit, bring about good things from it, care for the earth, and populate it (Genesis 1:28). While the command to populate the earth has not been restated for New Covenant believers, it is very obvious from numerous passages in the New Testament that we are called to bear fruit for the Lord in all we do for Him (Romans 7:4-6).

The covenant of marriage is one that can be broken if one of the partners pursues and entertains certain lusts that erode at the foundations upon which the covenant is based. Adultery is one; lust is another. As Malachi reveals, it is not just a matter of sexual adultery or sexual lust, but either of these manifesting in any forms within a relationship. Adultery and lust are present in more than just a sexual context, but in any context whereas someone or something places itself within a relationship, where it does not belong. Here in Malachi, we have the essence of why the covenant with God is compared to a marriage. Just as one can do these things to a marital relationship and it can be broken, one can pursue things that betray God, resulting in the break of covenant with Him.

In Malachi's day, marriages were arranged. They were not choices people made. This means that the priests were literally divorcing their wives and, through family arrangements, making agreements more advantageous to them with foreign women. Rather than upholding their covenants, they forsook them to pursue the idols of other nations. Not only did this break faith with their first spouses, but it also broke faith with God.

One way people reject and break the covenant with God is to chase after idols and foreign gods. While there is the literal sense in which people do this today by pursuing false gods available in other religions, there are more spiritual and figurative senses in which people marry and attach themselves unto foreign gods almost daily. We see numerous idols propagated in the church today:

- The pursuit of money, rooted in the love of money.

- The idolatry of family life above that of God, where the family unit becomes a cold and pursuing idol as headed by male figures.

- The pursuit of ministry to the exclusion of God.

- Uniting oneself to racist or sexist propaganda.

- The use of religion and religious ritual to distract one from obedience to God or genuinely learning what the will of God is for one's life.

- The abuse of God's Name by serving as a leader out of a sense of desired control, obtained in mistreating those one leads or covers.

Here in Malachi, we see those who started out on a right path but have attached themselves to false gods. Such was cause to be cut off from God's people, as they violated the covenant. There was no question their actions broke faith with God. They were no longer fit to participate in the Levitical covenant, as they could no longer rightly represent covenant relationship. We cannot go to God, complain because we fail to uphold covenant relationships with Him and others, and expect Him to accept what we offer in vain.

God makes it very clear how the leaders have broken their covenantal relationships: by ending their marriages with their wives, who were women of the covenant, and taking unto themselves other idolatrous women. Not only was this a stab against their wives, but it was also yet another disregard for the covenant of God. By uniting themselves unto foreign women, they likewise united themselves unto their pagan practices.

There is much found throughout in the Old Testament discouraging marriage with those who do not follow the true God. More than anything, God desires His people to follow Him completely. We cannot do this if we spend so much time trying to make something work, especially contradictory faiths or ideas. In modern times, interfaith marriages can work, but they take a great deal of effort and time, and statistics cite they are more likely to end in divorce.[57] So, looking at this, what do we do when interfaith religion is involved in a relationship?

Christians are discouraged from mixing worship systems, especially with non-believers. The mixing of pagan and Christian systems is an "unequal yoke" (2 Corinthians 2:14-18). This terminology translates to an imbalanced burden, one that causes both ideologies to present an unequal union. This passage isn't specifically about marriages, however. If anything, while the New Testament doesn't encourage interfaith marriage, it doesn't prohibit it, either. What it does teach is that the unbelieving spouse is sanctified by the believing spouse (1 Corinthians 7:14). Therefore, the requirement is that a believing spouse remains a believer – so they can influence their spouse from a spiritual perspective. It should not be that the unbelieving spouse influences the believer away from their faith, nor should the two comingle their beliefs to create a hybrid spirituality. In agreement, the two agree that the believing spouse has every right to their faith and they agree to whatever disagreements they have for the sake of maintaining a stability together (Amos 3:3).

Why is mixing spiritual systems prohibited? One must first understand the pagan viewpoint of the world. In pagan view, the material realm is only a means by which to manipulate the spiritual realm. Everything that is present on earth, in nature and in people, is a means to obtain something from the spiritual occult (hidden) world. It is for this reason paganism seems infiltrated into every aspect of the material realm: spells using alchemy and various elemental reactions, the use of nature and the worship thereof, focus on the seasons, and sexual rites. These various aspects of pagan worship give great insight into the way pagans view spirituality. It is for this reason that engaging in relationship with a pagan breaks covenant with God.

Many are unaware the prohibitions on relationships with temple prostitutes were about far more than prohibiting illicit sexual relationships (Acts 15:29, 1 Corinthians 6:12-18, 1 Thessalonians 4:3, Revelation 21:8). In paganism, sex (especially with a temple prostitute or as part of a pagan ritual) was about uniting oneself to the occult spiritual realm for a desired goal. To engage with a temple prostitute was to engage in a ritual designed to unite one with the demonic. Such participation makes the statement that one believes in the power of demons and occult rites to bring about certain desired effects. It's not a simple matter of having a little fun but cavorting with demons.

For a leader within God's house to marry a pagan woman

was the equivalent of consorting with a temple prostitute. In taking wives who worshipped foreign gods, these men were uniting themselves not just to those women, but to their pagan beliefs and practices as well. As those who were leaders, it sent a strong message to the congregation: it is not only acceptable, but desirable, to unite with demons. Such creates a bond of oneness out of God's will, resulting in ungodly offspring. Ungodly offspring are born both in a procreative sense and a spiritual one. These men were not simply following a different woman; they were participating in pagan rites and uniting themselves to these women, making commitments to them, through them, and abiding by the precepts these women lived, believed, and embraced!

Why would they do this? There are probably many reasons, some of which aren't that different from the idolatries they chase today. Marriages in ancient times were about alliances between families. Marrying a pagan might have meant better connections, fighting against a common enemy, larger territory, or better income. They weren't leaving their wives out of love or romance, but a sense that life could be better with someone else. The disciplines of Hebrew worship seemed pale, dry, even boring compared to what they felt awaited them on the other side of a divorce.

The reality of life is that at some point in time, their new marriages would cease to be exciting. They would be ordinary life, complete with their own challenges. The only difference would be they no longer had their own spiritual or national identities anymore, and they wouldn't find the true God in their idolatrous systems.

God hates the abandonment of covenant, as we can see here. He does not take pleasure when people find they cannot live together. God's words here are not specifically geared at general congregation leaders, but members and leaders. Divorce stands as a symbol of the covenant, which was broken in commitment to both their wives and their Creator.

We are also told God hates those who clothe themselves in violence, draping themselves in such ways of living and leading others. Violence is also a breaking of the covenant. We are told repeatedly that peace is a key principle for believers to live by and abide. If a leader engages in violence, it suggests violence is desirable and divine in principle to a congregation. On the contrary, violence is contrary to God's will for us. (Numbers 6:26, Psalm 37:11, Psalm 85;10, Isaiah 9:6, Matthew 5:9, Mark 9:50).

Violence in leadership is not just a violent application or isolated action in one's lifestyle. There is no question that, judging by the conduct of the leaders in their personal lives, they were individuals who were also abusive in their ministries. While God calls leaders to stand in ministry, He does not give them license to be abusive to those they lead. Covering and leadership are not opportunities to mistreat, beat down, or degrade other human beings. Leaders who abuse those under them are in violation of God's covenant and therefore break the connection they have with those who've served under their ministries.

Many leaders believe they are called to create disciples in their own image, rather than encouraging leaders to become what God has for them to be. The not-so-subtle, "I'm the leader, you're not" attitude prevails through an attitude of intimidation and insult present in many ministries. People feel they are unable to question, think, expand, or inquire about anything their minister may tell them. The result of such questions is condemnation and criticism, with the leader telling the individual they do not have the right to do such, and they are not ascribing to God's established order. Such thinking is irrational and in clear violation of God's leadership covenant command to bring forth life and peace. Ministers do not have a right to be violent through criticism or intimidation, nor do they have the right to cover with violence, even in the face of disobedience or insubordination.

We forget ministry is not made in a pulpit. It's a great thing to be able to get up in front of a group of people and command the audience. Preaching is a powerful way to proclaim the Gospel and is powerful when it impacts lives. The ability to do this, however, is not the way a ministry is made. Ministry is a literal work of stewardship. Ministers called to serve in God's house are called to serve Him by serving His people. While this doesn't mean ministers must live to be walked on or abused, it does mean a leader's mindset is not to be abusive or controlling. Ministry is about creating disciples and establishing leaders who can create disciples. To accomplish this, ministry becomes about impacting people's lives. If a true minister has nowhere to publicly preach, God will lead them to someone who needs God's touch in their lives. Ministers work with people out of the pulpit as much as the work with them in the pulpit. If a minister does not seek to connect and empower individual people as much as they seek to impact groups, they will never be effective in what they do. Covering with violence deters people away from ministry and, in the process, from God and true discipleship.

We conclude this section by learning how essential it is to guard ourselves in spirit (being spiritually protected, bearing the full armor of God, and being fully prepared for any spiritual battle we may encounter) and refrain from breaking faith. In so doing, leaders establish the principle that God's will is for His people to keep their commitments, their covenants with Him and one another, and are better prepared for spiritual battle as they have watched the precept of denying temptations through the good example of their leaders (Ephesians 6:10-17).

Malachi 2:17

You have wearied the LORD with your words.
"How have we wearied Him?" you ask.
By saying, "All who do evil are good in the eyes of the LORD, and He is pleased with them" or "Where is the God of justice?"

(Related Bible references: Isaiah 5:20, Isaiah 43:24, Jeremiah 17:15)

Malachi 2 ends with a statement on the hypocrisy of man and the way errant leaders have wearied God with their statements. It is not uncommon to hear people lament the woes of this world and, at the same time, criticize God for His lack of involvement in human affairs. Such leaders weary God for both failing to understand His ways and, at the same time, contribute to the problem through poor leadership. Not only do they do nothing to help solve problems, they contribute to them at the same time.

Christians are called to be a just people, and leadership is called to be just in its model of leadership. Leaders are also called to be models of God's justice as they are able. When a leader fails to uphold covenant leadership principles, they are not modeling the greater precepts of divine justice. God is not to blame for human wrongdoing, or for the sinfulness of humankind. It is the place of leaders to stand up to error and show it forth for what it is. Leaders are called to work for the necessary changes that reflect the Kingdom of God. The Kingdom of God begins within each of us as we repent from our sins and turn toward God (Luke 17:20-21).

Chapter 3

REPENT FROM FINANCIAL DECEPTION!
(MALACHI CHAPTER 3)

Key verses

- **Verse 1:** *"See, I will send My messenger, who will prepare the way before Me. Then suddenly the Lord you are seeking will come to His temple; the Messenger of the covenant, whom You desire, will come," says the LORD Almighty.*

- **Verse 2:** *But who can endure the day of his coming? Who can stand when He appears? For He will be like a refiner's fire or a launderer's soap.*

- **Verse 6:** *I the LORD do not change. So you, O descendants of Jacob, are not destroyed.*

- **Verse 8-9:** *"Will a man rob God? Yet you rob Me. "But you ask, 'How do we rob you?'" "In tithes and offerings. You are under a curse—the whole nation of you—because you are robbing Me.*

- **Verse 17:** *"They will be mine," says the LORD Almighty, "in the day when I make up My treasured possession. I will spare them, just as in compassion a man spares his son who serves him.*

Words and terms to know

- **Send**: From the Hebrew word *shalach* which means "to send, send away, let go, stretch out."[1]

- **Messenger**: From the Hebrew word *mal'ak* which means "messenger, representative."[2]

- **Prepare**: From the Hebrew word *panah* which means "to turn."[3]

- **Way**: From the Hebrew word *derek* which means "way, road, distance, journey, manner."[4]

- **Lord**: From the Hebrew word *'adown* which means "firm, strong, lord, master."[5]

- **Seeking**: From the Hebrew word *baqash* which means "to seek, require, desire, exact, request."[6]

- **Temple**: From the Hebrew word *heykal* which means "palace, temple, nave, sanctuary."[7]

- **Desire**: From the Hebrew word *chaphets* which means "desiring, delighting in, having pleasure in."[8]

- **Endure**: From the Hebrew word *kuwl* which means "to seize, contain, measure."[9]

- **Day of His coming**: From two Hebrew words: *yowm* which means "day, time, year"[10]; and *bow'* which means "to go in, enter, come, go, come in."[11]

- **Stand**: From the Hebrew word *'amad* which means "to stand, remain, endure, take one's stand."[12]

- **Refiner's fire**: From two Hebrew words: *tsaraph* which means "to smelt, refine, test;"[13] and *'esh* which means "fire."[14]

- **Launderer's soap**: From two Hebrew words: *kabac* which means "to wash (by treading), be washed, perform the work of a fuller;"[15] and *boriyth* which means "lye, potash, soap, alkai (which is used in laundering."[16]

- **Purifier**: From the Hebrew word *taher* which means "to be clean, be pure."[17]

- **Righteousness**: From the Hebrew word *tsedquah* which means, "justice, righteousness."[18]

- **Judgment**: From the Hebrew word *mishpat* which means "judgment, justice, ordinance."[19]

- **Sorcerers**: From the Hebrew word *kashaph* which means "To practice witchcraft or sorcery, use witchcraft."[20]

- **Adulterers**: From the Hebrew word *na'aph* which means "to commit adultery."[21]

- **Perjurers**: From two Hebrew words: *shequer* which means "lie, deception, disappointment, falsehood;"[22] and *shaba*, which means, "to swear, adjure."[23]

- **Defraud/Oppress**: From the Hebrew word *ashaq* which means "to press upon, oppress, violate, defraud, do violence, get deceitfully, wrong, exhort."[24]

- **Deprive**: From the Hebrew word *natah* which means "to stretch out, to extend, spread out, pitch, turn, pervert, incline, bend, bow."[25]

- **Change**: From the Hebrew word *shanah* which means "to repeat, do again, change, alter."[26]

- **Destroyed**: From the Hebrew word *kalah* which means "to accomplish, cease, consume, determine, end, fail, finish, be complete, be accomplished, be ended, be at an end, be finished, be spent."[27]

- **Return**: From the Hebrew word *shuwb* which means "to return, turn back."[28]

- **Rob**: From the Hebrew word *qaba* which means "to rob."[29]

- **Tithes**: From the Hebrew word *ma'aser* which means "tithe, tent part."[30]

- **Offerings**: From the Hebrew word *teruwmah* which means "contribution, offering."[31]

- **Storehouse**: From the Hebrew word *'owtsar* which means "treasure, storehouse."[32]

- **Test**: From the Hebrew word *bachan* which means "to examine, try, prove."[33]

- **Floodgates of heaven**: From two Hebrew words: *'arubbah* which means "lattice, window, sluice;"[34] and *shayamim* which means "heaven, heavens, sky."[35]

- **Blessed**: From the Hebrew word *berakah* which means "blessing; source of blessing; blessing, prosperity; blessing, praise of God; a gift, present; a treaty of peace."[36]

- **Delightful land**: From two Hebrew words: *chephets* which means "delight, pleasure;"[37] and *'erets* which means "land, earth."[38]

- **Harsh**: From the Hebrew word *chazaq* which means "to strengthen, prevail, harden, be strong, become strong, be courageous, be firm, grow firm, be resolute, be sore."[39]

- **Futile**: From the Hebrew word *shav'* which means "emptiness, vanity, falsehood."[40]

- **Arrogant**: From the Hebrew word *zed* which means "arrogant, proud, insolent, presumptious."[41]

- **Evildoers**: From two Hebrew words: *'asah* which means "to do, fashion, accomplish, make; (Piel) to press, squeeze;"[42] and *rish'ah* which means "wickedness, guilt."[43]

- **Prosper**: From the Hebrew word *banah* which means "to build, rebuild, establish, cause to continue."[44]

- **Challenge**: From the Hebrew word *bachan* which means "to examine, try, prove."[45]

- **Scroll of remembrance**: From two Hebrew words: *cepher* which means "book; missive, document, writing, book;"[46] and *zikrown* which means "memorial, reminder, rememberance."[47]

- **Treasured possession**: From the Hebrew word *cegullah* which means "possession, property."[48]

- **Compassion**: From the Hebrew word *chamal* which means "to spare, pity, have compassion on."[49]

- **Distinction**: From the Hebrew word *ra'ah* which means "to see, look at, inspect, perceive, consider."[50]

- **Righteous**: From the Hebrew word *tsaddiyq* which means "just, lawful, righteous."[51]

- **Wicked**: From the Hebrew word *rasha'* which means "wicked, criminal."[52]

Malachi 3:1-5

"See, I will send My messenger, Who will prepare the way before Me. Then suddenly the Lord you are seeking will come to His temple; the Messenger of the covenant, Whom you desire, will come," says the LORD Almighty.
But who can endure the day of His coming? Who can stand when He appears? For He will be like a refiner's fire or a launderer's soap. He will sit as a refiner and purifier of silver; He will purify the Levites and refine them like gold and silver. Then the LORD will have men who will bring offerings in righteousness, and the offerings of Judah and Jerusalem will be acceptable to the LORD, as in days gone by, as in former years.
"So I will come near to you for judgment. I will be quick to testify against sorcerers, adulterers and perjurers, against those who defraud laborers of their wages, who oppress the widows and the fatherless, and deprive aliens of justice, but do not fear Me," says the LORD Almighty.

(Related Bible references: Matthew 11:10, Luke 1:76, Isaiah 40:3, Isaiah 63:9, Haggai 2:7, Revelation 6:17, Isaiah 4:4, Matthew 3:10, Isaiah 1:25, 1 Peter 2:5, Zechariah 5:4, James 5:4)

Malachi chapter 3 opens with a dual message, both promise and warning. Within the promise we find the hope of the One Who was and is to come, Jesus Christ. We learn He is the messenger of the New Covenant, God's covenant of grace, which was sought all throughout the Old Testament for four thousand years. In Christ, we find the great promise of all prophecy and salvation. It is Him we long for, seek, and await.

The passage also refers to the one to come before Jesus, the righteous messenger, John the Baptist. John's presence here, while in minimal reference, is relevant when we consider John's position. While John marked the end of the prophetic era of the Old Covenant (Matthew 11:13), John also was a powerful type of the apostle to come in the New Covenant. Throughout Malachi we've seen references to God's messengers and those who bring forth God's word of correction in their day and age. John the Baptist brought forth correction to the leaders, proclaiming repentance as Christ was to come, and it is no accident he is mentioned here. On the outskirts of conventional religion, John's unique position gave him the ability to prepare the way for Christ in the hearts, minds, and beliefs of people. John the Baptist forged a paradigm shift whereby the people of his day were called to change their ways as a new era began in the Kingdom of God under Christ. Today the same is happening as God's people are called to shift, yet again, as Christ is about to return, and begin His transformational reign. While Malachi is a word for all leaders, it is a powerful word for God's apostles to stand up and issue necessary correction rather than sitting by or participating in it. Malachi constantly reminds the leaders of God to be different rather than just doing things that may look different. We also must never disregard the leaders who are different, who are a little on the outskirts, who are in many ways different from the "norm," because they come bearing a powerful...and different...message.

While the coming of Jesus Christ is a blessed and hopeful event, many do not consider Christ's coming is for judgment as much as it is for blessing. When Christ returns, everything and everyone wrong in this world will have to stand up be accountable. We learn it will be a time that some will be unable to endure. If we study further in Malachi 3, we learn one such group unable to stand at the Second Coming: those who have broken the Levitical covenant of leadership.

The mention of Jesus Christ in Malachi 3 may seem strange to some but comes as a powerful reference. There is hope in Christ's coming as much as there is judgment, and He does have the answers to the different things ministers face and that people in this world face. Jesus was also the perfect messenger of the Levitical Covenant, representing what solid covenant leadership was to be, do, act, think, and speak. Christ is peace, He is life and was not just one pointing to the covenant: He in Himself was and is the covenant. If we live in Christ, we are given everything we need to walk in life, peace, and grace to be positive representatives of the covenant of leadership. Jesus does not serve as an excuse, a means to do whatever we may like, or a cover by which we can behave badly. Jesus is not just our Savior, and not just our Redeemer, but also our Leader and our perfect example of all leadership can and should offer. Those in leadership who are called to represent Christ have the responsibility to answer to Him as well.

Jesus' mention is for this purpose: to speak of the judgment coming upon those leaders who misrepresent all He is. He is described as both a "refiner's fire" and "launderer's soap."

If we study what refiner's fire and launderer's soap are, we can gain insight into what leaders are to learn here in this passage:

- A refiner was one who worked with precious metals (predominately gold and silver). The goal of a refiner's fire was to purify the precious metals, and this was done using extremely hot fires. Metals were melted down, which would burn away or remove impurities in the process. Heating up the metal at such high temperatures brought it to a state of complete purification, giving such metals their rare and precious value.

- Launderer's soap (sometimes called fuller's soap) is a cleansing soap used to whiten and brighten dirty clothing. Launderer's soap is far more than simple detergent used in household washing machines; it is heavy-duty, harsh soap used on the toughest and dirtiest stains.[53] In Biblical times, it was used on garments and textile fabrics that needed rigorous or intensive cleaning. This is the sole reference to launderer's soap found anywhere in the Scriptures.

- The use of these two words is a Hebrew parallelism, done to point out the same attribute in a different way. Malachi is speaking here of a purification process which occurs only through Jesus Christ.

Refiner's fire and launderer's soap are referenced here because they both bring about the same result of purification, even though they bring about purification through different means (2 Peter 1:7). We learn Christ purifies injustices and sins, washing and bringing out the purest of purity in every situation. It is He Who will purify leadership, either through their repentance or removal of the impure from office. Once purification has come, we can see the great result: the church will be purified, offerings in righteousness will be made once again, and the righteous glory of the church will be restored to its place, restoring it to its position prior to the invasion of false leaders.

Jesus, John, and Peter all warned of wolves in sheep's clothing to come into the church, offering teachings that may appeal to the flesh of followers, but offered no substance to their souls (Matthew 7:15-23, 2 Peter 2:1, 1 John 4:1). Throughout the book of Malachi, we have seen the corruption of the church through disordered leadership. Here we learn Jesus Christ, as judge, brings the ultimate purification the church needs to bring about a restored church, clean and pure, dressed in white (Revelation 7:9-15). This purification has already begun and continues through these times as all that is covered up is uncovered and every secret is made known (Matthew 10:26-27).

Because Christ is purifying the church, God will be quick to come near us in judgment. He will testify against all those who engage in practices against the Word: sorcerers, adulterers, perjurers, those who defraud laborers of their wages, who oppress the widows and the fatherless, and who deprive aliens of justice. It is obvious those who engage in magic or attempt to manipulate the spiritual world, those who commit adultery in all its forms, those who lie under oath, cheat people of what they have earned, oppress those who have a difficult start in life, or take advantage of those who are not natives to one's country are acting in ways opposed to God and will not reap the protection or defense of God. We can see further evidence that we can work with God or against Him through our behavior and the way we conduct ourselves. The ultimate evidence that we must choose to work with God is here: if we do not work with God, He will testify against us. Anyone who does the things mentioned above has no fear of God, and He cannot create a defense for such conduct.

Malachi 3:6-15

"I the LORD do not change. So you, O descendants of Jacob, are not destroyed. Ever since the time of your forefathers you have turned away from My decrees and have not kept them. Return to Me, and I will return to you," says the LORD Almighty. "But you ask, 'How are we to return?'

"Will a man rob God? Yet you rob Me. "But you ask, 'How do we rob You?' "In tithes and offerings. You are under a curse—the whole nation of you—because you are robbing Me. Bring the whole tithe into the storehouse, that there may be food in my house. Test Me in this," says the LORD Almighty, "and see if I will not throw open the floodgates of heaven and pour out so much blessing that you will not have room enough for it. I will prevent pests from devouring your crops, and the vines in your fields will not cast their fruit," says the LORD Almighty. "Then all the nations will call you blessed, for yours will be a delightful land," says the LORD Almighty.

"You have said harsh things against Me," says the LORD. "Yet you ask, 'What have we said against You?'

"You have said, 'It is futile to serve God. What did we gain by carrying out His requirements and going about like mourners before the LORD Almighty? But now we call the arrogant blessed. Certainly the evildoers prosper, and even those who challenge God escape.'"

(Related Bible references: Numbers 23:19, Romans 11:29, James 1:17, Lamentations 3:22, Acts 7:51, Zechariah 1:3, Zechariah 1:6, Nehemiah 13:10, Proverbs 3:9, 1 Chronicles 26:20, 2 Chronicles 31:11, Nehemiah 10:38, Genesis 7:11, 2 Kings 7:2, 2 Chronicles 31:10, Amos 4:9, Daniel 8:9, Job 21:14, Psalm 73:12, Psalm 95:9)

We further gain perspective on the nature of God and the sins of those who corrupt leadership beginning in verse 6. In Malachi 3, God further states His case against disordered leadership, specifically in the area of financial matters. Verse 6 opens with

God's statement of consistency: He does not change. While some today question the unchangeableness of God, we can clearly see here in Malachi, it is not God Who changes, it is humanity. We can see it was not God Who broke the covenant, but the leaders, as God was faithful to His promise (and the people were not destroyed). It was the leaders who turned from God's ways and united themselves with foreign women, foreign idols, engaged in dishonest practices (such as stealing and spiritual deception), and then turned around and questioned God for not accepting their practices.

The ultimate message threaded throughout Malachi is the call to repentance, present here in this passage. God is both warning and correcting leaders, telling them what needs to straighten up in their ministries and personal lives and warning them of what will happen if they fail to do so. If those who have left God will return to God, His blessing, providence, and protection will rest on them again (Deuteronomy 11:26-28).

Yet again, we see errant leaders question God: they ask, "How are we to return?" This question insults to God as the implication lies within it that such leaders have fallen and are unaware of their sins. It echoes back to Adam's lack of responsibility in the garden, when God called out to Him in the cool of the day and instead of coming forward, he ran and hid (Genesis 3:10-12). Trying to deny one's sins exist or pretending one does not know God's will, especially when one is a leader, is highly reprehensible. God, however, answers their false confusion with powerful words showing forth another way they wronged God and had abandoned the covenant through their conduct.

God raises a sensitive area of sin in Malachi 3 many would rather pretend does not exist: the issue of financial and moral fraud present in the church. Even though financial fraud in churches and ministries has come to the surface since the mid-1980s, many deny the reality that there are people who use the ministerial office to abuse, misuse, or fraud others. Reading Malachi eliminates any question that there are those who claim to have gifts or callings in the Lord, but work to fraud and steal from others. As we live in a world where this practice is rampant, we must develop necessary discernment to recognize the practice among us. Many misinterpret Malachi 3 to say something it indeed does not – and as people preparing for leadership, we must focus on the words of Malachi to learn both the facts and consequences of how ministers often seek to rob God.

The entire nation of Israel lived under a curse in Malachi's day because the tithes (the ten percent offering of one's income brought as an offering to the Lord) was not delivered to the Lord and His work but was stolen by the leaders. While many use this passage in defense of requiring congregation members to bring in tithes (using obvious guilt-inducing tactics in the process), they are mistranslating this passage to further theft of tithes from God.

According to the passage, the priests were holding back part of the tithes for themselves, as many ministers today are guilty of doing, in addition to other sins committed. We learn this is completely inappropriate – it is wrong to use God for financial gain in every circumstance and situation.

The facts speak for themselves: as in Malachi's day, some ministers today suffer from love of money. This study raises many interesting questions about the Biblical verse that tells us that the love of money is the root of all evil (1 Timothy 6:3-10). Money itself is not the root of all evil, but the love of money is the root of evil as a basic relationship one has in their life is with money.

Money and one's relationship with money is an essential aspect to existence because money is a fluid by which we are able to buy and sell. Money and the transfer of money is essential to survival in every culture worldwide. If one has a disordered relationship with money, there will be problems in every area of one's life. If ministry is added to this complicated situation, the result becomes disastrous. Such is evident in the fruit of ministries which may be financially lucrative but are spiritually and morally bankrupt.

I do not intend to suggest ministers are unworthy of receiving payment for their work as ministers. The Bible makes it clear the worker is worth his wages (Matthew 10:10, John

4:36) and when it is available, those who are taught should support those who teach them (1 Corinthians 9:1-22). The issue we address here is much deeper than taking a salary or not taking one. We are examining the issue of using a ministerial office for the expressed goal of personal financial gain. The purpose of ministry is not to make a financial windfall; it is to do the work of the Lord. Trusting that God provides all needs, leaders can be supported by the work they do; however, the work they do cannot support greed.

We learned in the last chapter the Levites were the only tribe of all twelve that did not receive a land inheritance, because God Himself was to be their inheritance (Joshua 13:33). Through the Levitical covenant, God kept and cared for the Levites and all their needs – but they had to trust in God instead of looking to material land or possessions for their security. This precept still holds true for Christian leaders today. Leaders must trust God for all they have and believe He will provide for all their needs in every situation. Sometimes this requires us to sacrifice the comforts of visual reassurance that needs will be met, operating instead on faith (Hebrews 11:1). While it is difficult at times, it challenges leaders to keep their senses about them; to remember their citizenship is heavenly, not earthly; and prove to be good stewards with every resource God gives (Matthew 8:20, Philippians 3:20-21, 1 Peter 4:9-11).

Even though the leaders are the ones who receive tithes, it is imperative ministers of the Gospel do not lose sight to Whom tithes truly belong. When living with a love of money, leaders tend to forget people bring their tithe to the Lord through the leaders, not just for the personal benefit of leaders. Leaders receive the benefit from tithes, buy only because the system of tithing is through God's establishment. Individuals who tithe are blessed by God for their obedience to God's system and their assistance to the function of God's church, not because they are giving to the benefit of a private individual. While ministers of all kinds may benefit personally from the tithes and offerings given to their ministries, the individual is not making a private donation into their minister's personal life but giving to God through the church or ministry they support financially.

It is for this reason that leaders must make the following explicitly clear: tithes are not given to an individual leader, such as one's pastor or apostle. Too often I hear people say, "You need to give your tithes to your pastor! Believe no one who tells you otherwise!" If we are specifically giving tithes with the intent to give to a personal individual, we are not giving tithes because we are not sowing into the work of God, but a person. Tithes are given to the church or ministry supporting, teaching, and nurturing the spiritual empowerment necessary for an individual to grow. It is there, thanks to God, for His gift of grace manifest and working through the grace and calling of the church or ministry they benefit from or attend.

At the same time, I have had many ask me, "What about people who did not give?" We can see throughout Malachi that the issue wasn't really a lack of things or people not presenting anything to leadership for tithes and offerings. The ball, so to speak, was dropped by the leaders, who kept the best part of the offerings for themselves and just presented what was left over to God. There is a question here, though that is important to raise: it is not acceptable to simply not give at all because of a bad leader or bad leadership. God commands His people to give, and that means if we find a leader or ministry to be of questionable financial integrity, we need to find a ministry to give unto that is not questionable in its practices. It would be easy to say that the people of Malachi's day were justified in simply not giving, but that's not the impression I get from the book of Malachi. What I do see here is a clear example of two facts:

- **It is relevant where we sow (give tithes and offerings)**: If you are giving with the attitude that "God can just come and find your tithe" and bless you despite the fact that you know you're giving to a false ministry or financially deceptive leader, God is not going to bless the offering like you might like. Why? We are specifically commanded to sow in good soil (Galatians 6:7-9). We reap what we partake in. If a ministry has a questionable circumstance, situation, or leader at the helm and you know about it, sowing into that ministry in the hopes it will go to the work of God won't work.

- **Giving is required**: There is no statement anywhere in Malachi that eliminates the responsibility for giving because of giving to an irresponsible circumstance. God's people are called to be always discerning and sow wisely. We can't exempt ourselves from giving because of bad situations, circumstances, or because we dislike someone somewhere else. Being in the right ministry at the right time requires us to give, both in and out of season.

Let's never forget that by His very nature, God gives. A central verse in Scripture, quoted frequently, tells us that God loved the world so much, He gave His only Son:

For God so loved the world that He gave His one and only Son, that whoever believes in Him shall not perish but have eternal life. (John 3:16).

God didn't look over the world and decide this gift was only for a select few. It wasn't about giving where it seemed most advantageous or attention-worthy. As believers, giving is part of our nature – both leaders and followers. We have the right to be discerning about where we give, but we don't have the right – no matter our position in church – to refrain from giving.

Instead of just telling people they don't have to give anymore, God demands the leaders of Malachi put Him to the test: allow His people to bring in the tithes, bring those tithes to God, and watch for the abundance of blessing He will pour out! If leaders simply abide by God's precepts, He will bless in abundance. If anyone has doubts, God invites leaders to fully place their trust in Him and test His goodness and grace toward them. There will be more than enough for all: the ministers, the congregations, and the poor and needy, who we must bless in our abundance from God (Exodus 23:11, Leviticus 19:15, Leviticus 25:35, Luke 14:13-14).

God also promises to protect crops and sustenance among those who follow His precepts. This does not just imply help in an agricultural sense, but in a modern sense as well: God will protect all the resources that come in and help life and work in ministry. Rather than having to live concerned about scandals, true leaders can trust God will provide and protect what He has given. When God has given, nobody can take it away. It is for this reason that all nations will recognize the church as blessed: God will give to the church, and it will remain as the blessing of the church, and many will stand in awe of God's goodness and desire to learn more about Him and His goodness (Matthew 5:13-14).

God continues His points against the leadership, making His final point: they have said harsh words against Him, describing ministry work as futile. This final point shows the great disregard and disrespect the ministry leaders had for God and His work. In pursuit of all the wrong things, they harbored resentment for the sacrifices, lifestyle, and ethics ministry life demands. At the same time, they were not living according to God's precepts and not reaping His benefits in their efforts to obtain worldly desires and pursue worldly things. Leaders of every time, including this one, must realize if they want to receive God's blessings for ministry, they must walk in obedience to the Father in every area of life. They cannot buy into deceptive concepts of blessing, where one looks solely to worldly concepts to define blessing. While evildoers may seem to flourish for a time, the evildoers will not prosper, and those who challenge God will never escape (Genesis 38:10, Job 11:20, Job 18:5, Psalm 9:5, Psalm 32:10, Proverbs 10:7, 2 Thessalonians 2:8-12).

Malachi 3:16-18

Then those who feared the LORD talked with each other, and the LORD listened and heard. A scroll of remembrance was written in His presence concerning those who feared the LORD and honored His Name.

TURNING THE HEARTS OF THE LEADERS TOWARD THE FATHER

"They will be Mine," says the LORD Almighty, "In the day when I make up My treasured possession. I will spare them, just as in compassion a man spares his son who serves him. And you will again see the distinction between the righteous and the wicked, between those who serve God and those who do not.

(Related Bible references: Psalm 66:16, Hebrews 3:13, Psalm 56:8, Isaiah 65:6, Revelation 20:12, Exodus 19:5, Deuteronomy 7:6, Psalm 135:4, Isaiah 62:3, Psalm 103:13, Psalm 58:11)

Malachi 3 ends with a separation of the leaders into two camps: those who would fear the Lord and follow His ways, and those who would not. Even though all are given the same opportunity for repentance, not everyone will make the choice to follow God. We see this reality all throughout the Scriptures (Genesis 7:1, Jeremiah 5:3, Jeremiah 8:6, Matthew 3:2, Mark 6:12, Luke 13:3, Acts 2:38, Acts 3:19). It is obvious some of the ministers in Malachi's day preferred their own ways, for whatever their reasons might have been. We never hear of them again, because they made their own choice, to be cut off from the ministry and presence of God.

Some turned away, but some also turned toward the Lord, and those who chose the Lord gathered to speak with one another. This process of speech was frequent, rather than a one-time event. They discussed the precepts of God and all He revealed through the oracle of Malachi. We learn a scroll of remembrance, documenting those who would fear the Lord and commit to His ways, was written. This served to remind those present and future generations that faithfulness to the Lord was to remain a perpetual ordinance.

This passage opens the dialogue between God and the leaders to the leaders and the people. The decision to fear the Lord and serve Him does not just fall on leaders, but to everyone within the Kingdom of God. Dialogue between God, leaders, and congregants is essential to solid Kingdom function. It's inappropriate to think leaders are the only ones with the right to speak. Leaders and congregants must speak often about what God is doing, revealing, and correcting on a regular basis.

Within the bounds of decency and order, group studies, sessions, meetings, and other events should be held to foster Kingdom communication. This does not give congregants or leaders the right to control matters, but to follow God's precepts for sharing with one another in Kingdom principles.

Due to ministry abuses, this essential dialogue most likely broke down as violent leaders ordered the people of God around and about. How many ministries today evidence the same issues? No one can speak to some leaders about anything, let alone dialogue with them. Leaders able to dialogue prove their solid ministries as they share with others about God and receive what God has revealed to others as well.

Still, conversation was necessary, and some discussions must be had to bring about unity. We can't reach the point of Christian unity without the hard conversations. We unite in truth to see such is precious in God's sight. Psalm 133:1-3 sings of this sentiment:

How good and pleasant it is
  when God's people live together in unity!
It is like precious oil poured on the head,
  running down on the beard,
running down on Aaron's beard,
  down on the collar of his robe.
It is as if the dew of Hermon
  were falling on Mount Zion.
For there the Lord bestows His blessing,
  even life forevermore.

It is obvious that God has come forth to take His church back. We are to belong to Him again, not chasing after aspirations that don't enhance church life. God promises those who follow His precepts will serve to be His treasured possession, valued above any worldly or earthly riches. God will spare those who are found in Him, and the righteous and wicked shall be divided, yet again. The standing difference between righteousness and unrighteousness is whether one serves God. Let today's leaders be those who stand up to be written in His scroll, and to be those who serve God in righteousness!

Chapter 4

THE COMING DAY OF JUDGMENT AND PROMISE
(MALACHI CHAPTER 4)

Key verses

- **Verse 1:** *"Surely the day is coming; it will burn like a furnace. All the arrogant and every evildoer will be stubble, and that day that is coming will set them on fire,"* says the LORD Almighty. *"Not a root or a branch will be left to them."*

- **Verse 2:** *But for you who revere My Name, the sun of righteousness will rise with healing in its wings. And you will go out and leap like calves released from the stall.*

- **Verse 5-6:** *"See, I will send you the prophet Elijah before that great and dreadful day of the LORD comes. He will turn the hearts of the fathers to their children, and the hearts of the children to their fathers; or else I will come and strike the land with a curse."*

Words and phrases to know

- **Day**: From the Hebrew word *yowm* which means "day, period of time, year."[1]

- **Coming**: From the Hebrew word *bow'* which means "to go in, enter, come, go, come in."[2]

- **Burn**: From the Hebrew word *ba'ar* which means "to burn, consume, kindle, be kindled; to be stupid, brutish, barbarous."[3]

- **Furnace**: From the Hebrew word *tannuwr* which means "furnace, oven, fire-pot, (portable) stove."[4]

- **Arrogant**: From the Hebrew word *zed* which means "arrogant, proud, insolent, presumptuous."[5]

- **Evildoer**: From two Hebrew words: *'asah* which means "to do, fashion, accomplish, make; to press, squeeze"[6]; and *rish'ah*, which means, "wickedness, guilt."[7]

- **Stubble**: From the Hebrew word *quash* which means "stubble, staff."[8]

- **Fire**: From the Hebrew word *lahat* which means "to burn, blaze, scorch, kindle, blaze up, flame."[9]

- **Root**: From the Hebrew word *sheresh* which means "root."[10]

- **Branch**: From the Hebrew word *anaph* which means "bough, branch."[11]

- **Revere**: From the Hebrew word *'yare* which means "fearing, reverent, afraid."[12]

- **Sun of righteousness**: From two Hebrew words: *shemesh* which means "sun"[13]; and *tsedaqah* which means "justice, righteousness."[14]

- **Healing**: From the Hebrew word *marpe'* which means "health, healing, cure."[15]

- **Wings**: From the Hebrew word *kanaph* which means "wing, extremity, edge, winged, border, corner, shirt."[16]

- **Leap**: From the Hebrew word *puwsh* which means "to spring about; (Niphal) to be scattered, to spread."[17]

- **Trample down**: From the Hebrew word *'acac* which means "to press, crush, press by treading, tread down or out, press (as in grapes)."[18]

- **Ashes**: From the Hebrew word *'epher* which means "ashes; worthlessness."[19]

- **Remember**: From the Hebrew word *zakar* which means "to remember, recall, call to mind."[20]

- **Fathers**: From the Hebrew word *'ab*, which means "father of an individual; of God as father of His people; head or founder of a household, group, family, or clan; ancestor; originator or patron of a class, profession, or art; of producer, generator; of benevolence and protection; term of respect and honor; ruler or chief."[21]

- **Children**: From the Hebrew word *ben* which means "son, grandson, child, member of a group."[22]

Malachi 4:1-6

"Surely the day is coming; it will burn like a furnace. All the arrogant and every evildoer will be stubble, and that day that is coming will set them on fire," says the LORD Almighty. "Not a

root or a branch will be left to them. But for you who revere My Name, the sun of righteousness will rise with healing in its wings. And you will go out and leap like calves released from the stall. Then you will trample down the wicked; they will be ashes under the soles of your feet on the day when I do these things," says the LORD Almighty.

"Remember the law of my servant Moses, the decrees and laws I gave him at Horeb for all Israel.

"See, I will send you the prophet Elijah before that great and dreadful day of the LORD comes. He will turn the hearts of the fathers to their children, and the hearts of the children to their fathers; or else I will come and strike the land with a curse."

(Related Bible references: Joel 2:31, 2 Peter 3:7, 2 Peter 3;8, Obadiah 1:18, Amos 2:9, Luke 1:78. Ephesians 5:14, Revelation 2:28, Micah 7:10, Exodus 20:3, Deuteronomy 4:10, Psalm 147:19, Matthew 11:14, Luke 1:17, Joel 2:31, Zechariah 14:12, Zechariah 5:3)

Malachi Chapter 4 parallels the beginning of Malachi chapter 3 in a certain sense. Some people believe it is speaking of the first coming of Jesus Christ, rather than speaking of the second coming. I believe this passage has elements of both events, paralleling the similarities between the two. Both the first and second comings of Christ are either blessings or great challenges for people. The first and second comings of Christ require decisions on the part of those who claim to be believers and especially require decisions on the part of Christian leaders. Christ's Word is final in both, and the result of Christ's comings is either great blessing or great punishment. As we now look to the second coming, we see elements of the second coming alive and active in this passage. As we are aware Jesus will return, we are also aware He will bring judgment. He shall judge the world in righteousness:

This will take place on the day when God judges people's secrets through Jesus Christ, as my gospel declares. (Romans 2:16)

TURNING THE HEARTS OF THE LEADERS TOWARD THE FATHER

In the presence of God and of Christ Jesus, Who will judge the living and the dead, and in view of His appearing and His kingdom... (2 Timothy 4:1)

We are given a very vivid picture of what will become of the evildoer and wicked: they will be reduced to stubble, nothing more than mere ash, because they will be set on fire (Mark 9:43-49, Luke 17:29, John 15:6, Jude 1:7). As we know from earlier passages in Malachi, fire is used as an image of purification:

For our God is a consuming fire. (Hebrews 12:29, KJV).

As the wicked cannot stand in righteousness, they must be removed in a process that purifies the church and roots out all unrighteousness. This purification will be brought about by the Holy Spirit:

Peter, an apostle of Jesus Christ, to the strangers scattered throughout Pontus, Galatia, Cappadocia, Asia, and Bithynia, Elect according to the foreknowledge of God the Father, through sanctification of the Spirit, unto obedience and sprinkling of the blood of Jesus Christ: Grace unto you, and peace, be multiplied. (1 Peter 1:1-2, KJV)

The secondary message in Malachi, aside from repentance, is hope for the righteous. The promise of every judgment is the hope of purification, which will bring us, once and for all, exactly where we need to be in Him. Malachi ends with the promise of obedience, the result of the fruits of righteous labor. Many believe righteousness is a waste in this life, with no purpose, result, or reward. No matter how one may feel now, righteousness does lead to life. Those who revere the Name of God and serve Him in righteousness and truth will rise in Christ, the Sun of Righteousness, our light and truth. Healing will come from every aspect of Christ and every extension, through His hands and even His garments. Those who suffer from health problems will see complete healing, and those who mourn now will have joy, knowing life and freedom. The healed will not just jump for joy, but scatter and disperse in joy, letting everyone know what God has done for them through the saving, healing, and complete redemptive work of Jesus Christ. Those who are righteous will trample down the wicked instead of experiencing the oppression of the wicked. The righteous will take the position of authority, and the wicked placed under their feet.

The righteous are bidden by God to remember the Word of God, present in the law of Moses. While we recognize Jesus was the fulfillment of the Law, that doesn't mean we cannot learn from those faithful words of life that guided believers for thousands of years. In all situations, we must hear God speaking to us, telling us to remember the fullness of His Word and all that is contained therein. Rather than look to the right or the left, we hear God commanding us now, as He does in Isaiah:

This is the way, walk ye in it! (Isaiah 30:32, KJV)

This echoes the words of Matthew 7:13-14:

Enter ye in at the strait gate: for wide is the gate, and broad is the way, that leadeth to destruction, and many there be which go in thereat: Because strait is the gate, and narrow is the way, which leadeth unto life, and few there be that find it. (KJV)

We follow a narrow path; one that excludes falling from one side to another. We are commanded to remain in the place of truth, centered in His will, embracing the fullness of life that He has for each and every one of us.

The final words in the book of Malachi tell us again of the one who is to come, the forerunner for Jesus Christ. These verses are the reason John the Baptist was mistaken to be a resurrected or reincarnated Elijah (Matthew 11:14, John 1:21-25). The people of Jesus' day firmly believed Elijah would literally return as the forerunner for the Messiah. In such acknowledgement, they were both acknowledging Jesus Christ as the Messiah and John as His forerunner. The one to come before Christ, John the Baptist, bore the prophetic anointing of Elijah. As the book of Malachi is geared toward leaders, every leader – especially those who are apostles – need to recognize themselves as the forerunners of the second coming of Jesus Christ. While not all are apostles in the sense of Malachi's or John's apostolic type or prophets in the sense of the prophetic office, every leader carries the Spirit of prophecy by testifying about Jesus Christ (Revelation 19:10). May all leaders bear His testimony, without bringing shame or reproach to His holy and divine Name. May they look to their Father, in heaven, and embrace His love and reflect His integrity in their lives. The hearts of the children shall be inclined toward their fathers, especially those in faith, and most especially, their heavenly Father. By extension, we can also see a final word here for leaders: the hearts of those in leadership, who teach in faith, shall be turned toward their congregations, and the congregations turned toward the leaders who lead in true righteousness. The leaders must first turn their hearts toward God, that the spiritual sons and daughters may turn right, in trust, toward the leaders. Those whose hearts are not turned will experience the absence of God's blessing, but those whose hearts turn shall reap life eternal and the full blessing of God, in an age void of sin, after the kingdoms of this world become the Kingdom of our Lord and of His Christ.

The seventh angel sounded his trumpet, and there were loud voices in heaven, which said:

> *"The kingdom of the world has become*
> *the kingdom of our Lord and of His Messiah,*
> *and He will reign for ever and ever."* (Revelation 11:15)

And into eternity, they shall reign forever and ever, Amen!

References

[1]Lambdin, Thomas O. <u>Gospel of Thomas, The</u>. Public Domain. http://www.sacred-texts.com/chr/thomas.htm. Accessed March 20, 2015.

Introduction references

- "Book of Malachi." http://www.bible.org/page.php?page_id=945
- "Book of Malachi, The." http://en.wikipedia.org/wiki/Book_of_Malachi

Chapter 1

[1] <u>Strong's Exhaustive Concordance of the Bible</u>, #4853
[2] Ibid., #4401
[3] Ibid, #0157
[4] Ibid., #6125
[5] Ibid., #7567
[6] Ibid., #1129
[7] Ibid., #1366
[8] Ibid., #7564
[9] Ibid., #1129
[10] Ibid., #2040
[11] Ibid., #0001

[12] Ibid., #3519
[13] Ibid., #0113
[14] Ibid., #4172
[15] Ibid., #3548
[16] Ibid., #9059
[17] Ibid., #1351
[18] Ibid., #3899
[19] Ibid., #4196
[20] Ibid., #5787
[21] Ibid., #6455
[22] Ibid., #2470
[23] Ibid., #6346
[24] Ibid., #7521
[25] Ibid., #5375
[26] Ibid., #1817
[27] Ibid., #0215
[28] Ibid., #2600
[29] Ibid., #4503
[30] Ibid., #1419
[31] Ibid., #2490
[32] Ibid., #4972
[33] Ibid., #5230
[34] Ibid., #3372
[35] "Edom." http://en.wikipedia.org/wiki/Edom. Accessed March 3, 2011.

Chapter 2

[1] <u>Strong's Exhaustive Concordance of the Bible</u>, #4687
[2] Ibid., #8085
[3] Ibid., #7760
[4] Ibid., #3820
[5] Ibid., #3994
[6] Ibid., #1293
[7] Ibid., #1605
[8] Ibid., #2233
[9] Ibid., #6569
[10] Ibid., #5375
[11] Ibid., #1285
[12] Ibid., #2416
[13] Ibid., #7965
[14] Ibid., #3372

15. Ibid., #4334
16. Ibid., #7725
17. Ibid., #5771
18. Ibid., #8193
19. Ibid., #8104
20. Ibid., #1847
21. Ibid., #8451
22. Ibid., #4397
23. Ibid., #3782
24. Ibid., #7843
25. Ibid., #0959
26. Ibid., #8217
27. Ibid., #5375
28. Ibid., #8451
29. Ibid., #0898
30. Ibid., #2490
31. Ibid., #6944
32. Ibid., #1166
33. Ibid., #5236
34. Ibid, #0410
35. Ibid., #3680
36. Ibid., #1832
37. Ibid., #1065
38. Ibid., #0603
39. Ibid., #5749
40. Ibid., #0259
41. Ibid., #0430
42. Ibid., #2233
43. Ibid., #0802
44. Ibid., #5271
45. Ibid., #8104
46. Ibid., #7307
47. Ibid., #7971
48. Ibid., #3680
49. Ibid., #2555
50. Ibid., #3830
51. Ibid., #4941
52. "Levite." http://en.wikipedia.org/wiki/Levite
53. Ibid.
54. Ibid.

⁵⁵ "Covenant." <u>The American Heritage Dictionary</u>, http://education.yahoo.com/reference/dictionary/entry/covenant. Accessed March 7, 2009.
⁵⁶ Ibid.
⁵⁷ "Interfaith Marriages Lead To More Divorce." http://www.divorcereform.org/mel/rinterfaith.html. Accessed March 8, 2009.

Chapter 3

¹ <u>Strong's Exhaustive Concordance of the Bible</u>, #7971
² Ibid., #4397
³ Ibid., #6437
⁴ Ibid., #1870
⁵ Ibid., #0113
⁶ Ibid., #1245
⁷ Ibid., #1964
⁸ Ibid., #2655
⁹ Ibid., #3557
¹⁰ Ibid., #3117
¹¹ Ibid., #0935
¹² Ibid., #5795
¹³ Ibid., #6884
¹⁴ Ibid., #0784
¹⁵ Ibid., #3526
¹⁶ Ibid., #1287
¹⁷ Ibid., #2891
¹⁸ Ibid., #6666
¹⁹ Ibid., #4941
²⁰ Ibid., #3784
²¹ Ibid., #5003
²² Ibid., #8267
²³ Ibid., #7650
²⁴ Ibid., #6231
²⁵ Ibid., #5186
²⁶ Ibid., #8138
²⁷ Ibid., #3615
²⁸ Ibid., #7725
²⁹ Ibid., #6906
³⁰ Ibid., #4643
³¹ Ibid., #8641
³² Ibid., #0214

[33] Ibid., #0974
[34] Ibid., #0699
[35] Ibid., #8064
[36] Ibid., #1293
[37] Ibid., #2656
[38] Ibid., #0776
[39] Ibid., #2388
[40] Ibid., #7723
[41] Ibid., #2086
[42] Ibid., #6213
[43] Ibid., #7564
[44] Ibid., #1129
[45] Ibid., #0974
[46] Ibid., #5612
[47] Ibid., #2146
[48] Ibid., #5459
[49] Ibid., #2550
[50] Ibid., #7200
[51] Ibid., #6662
[52] Ibid., #7563
[53] "What Is Fuller's Soap?" http://www.ehow.com/about_4572172_what-fullers-soap.html. Accessed March 22, 2009.

Chapter 4

[1] <u>Strong's Exhaustive Concordance of the Bible</u>, #3117
[2] Ibid., #0935
[3] Ibid., #1197
[4] Ibid., #8574
[5] Ibid., #2086
[6] Ibid., #6213
[7] Ibid., #7564
[8] Ibid., #7179
[9] Ibid., #3857
[10] Ibid., #8328
[11] Ibid., #6057
[12] Ibid., #3373
[13] Ibid., #8121
[14] Ibid., #6666
[15] Ibid., #4832
[16] Ibid., #3671

[17] Ibid., #6335
[18] Ibid., #6072
[19] Ibid., #0665
[20] Ibid., #2142
[21] Ibid., #0001
[22] Ibid., #1121

About the Author

Dr. Lee Ann B. Marino, Ph.D., D.Min., D.D.

DR. LEE ANN B. MARINO, PH.D., D.MIN., D.D. (she/her) is "everyone's favorite theologian" leading Gen X, Millennials, and Gen Z with expertise in leadership training, queer and feminist theology, general religion, and apostolic theology. She has served in ministry since 1998 and was ordained as a pastor in 2002 and an apostle in 2010. She founded what is now Sanctuary Apostolic Fellowship Empowerment (SAFE)
Ministries in 2004. Under her ministry heading Dr. Marino is founder and Overseer of Sanctuary International Fellowship Tabernacle (SIFT) (the original home of National Coming Out Sunday) and The Sanctuary Network, and Chancellor of Apostolic Covenant Theological Seminary (ACTS).

Affectionately nicknamed "the Spitfire," Dr. Marino has spent over two decades as an "apostle, preacher, and teacher" (2

Timothy 1:11), exercising her personal mandate to become "all things to all people" (1 Corinthians 9:22). Her embrace of spiritual issues (both technical and intimate) has found its home among both seekers and believers, those who desire spiritual answers to today's issues.

Dr. Marino has preached throughout the United States, Puerto Rico, and Europe in hundreds of religious services and experiences throughout the years. A history maker in her own right, she has spent over two decades in advocacy, education, and work for and within minority spiritual communities (including African American, Hispanic, and LGBTQ+). She has also served as the first woman on all-male synods, councils, and panels, as well as the first preacher or speaker welcomed of a different race, sexual orientation, or identity among diverse communities. Today, Dr. Marino's work extends to over 150 countries as she hosts the popular *Kingdom Now* podcast, which is in the top 20 percentile of all podcasts worldwide. She is also the author of over 35 books and the popular Patheos column, *Leadership on Fire*. To date, she has had five bestselling titles within their subject matter: *Understanding Demonology, Spiritual Warfare, Healing, and Deliverance: A Manual for the Christian Minister*; *Ministry School Boot Camp: Training for Helps Ministries, Appointments, and Beyond*; *Discovering Intimacy: A Journey Through the Song of Solomon*; *Fruit of the Vine: Study and Commentary on the Fruit of the Spirit*; and *Ministering to LGBTQ+ (and Those Who Love Them): A Primer for Queer Theology* (and its accompanying workbook).

As a public icon and social media influencer, Dr. Marino advocates healthy body image (curvy/full-figured), representation as a demisexual/aromantic, and albinism awareness as a model. Known to those she works with, she is a spiritual mom, teacher, leader, professor, confidant, and friend. She continues to transform, receiving new teaching, revelation, and insight in this thing we call "ministry." Through years of spiritual growth and maturity, Dr. Marino stands as herself, here to present what God has given to her for any who have an ear to hear.

TURNING THE HEARTS OF THE LEADERS TOWARD THE FATHER

For more information, visit her website at kingdompowernow.org.

www.ingramcontent.com/pod-product-compliance
Lightning Source LLC
Chambersburg PA
CBHW060847050426
42453CB00008B/870